Elixir of Empire

D1437973

Also from Westphalia Press

westphaliapress.org

Elixir of Empire

The English Public Schools, Ritualism, Freemasonry, and Imperialism

by P. J. Rich

*By degrees 'the public school spirit'
became one of the most potent
of the imperial elixirs.*
–A. P. Thornton

WESTPHALIA PRESS
An imprint of Policy Studies Organization

Westphalia Press
An imprint of Policy Studies Organization
1527 New Hampshire Ave., NW
Washington, D.C. 20036
info@ipsonet.org

ISBN-13: 978-1633910393
ISBN-10: 1633910393

Cover design by Taillefer Long at Illuminated Stories:
www.illuminatedstories.com

Daniel Gutierrez-Sandoval, Executive Director
PSO and Westphalia Press

Devin Proctor, Director of Media and Publications
PSO and Westphalia Press

Updated material and comments on this edition
can be found at the Westphalia Press website:
www.westphaliapress.org

Oriel Window, Eton. A magnificent display of heraldic stained glass in the College Hall. Not only North American Indians cherished tokens and totems. Public schools, whose connections with heraldry have received little attention, provided symbolic experiences that influenced the rituals of the Imperial mandarins.

Elixir of Empire

*The English Public Schools,
Ritualism, Freemasonry, and Imperialism*

Second Edition
*Volume One in the trilogy English Public
Schools and Ritualistic Imperialism*

Dr. Paul Rich, Honorary Research Fellow of The University of Western Australia, was elected to the Royal Historical Society (London) in 1992, and to the Royal Society of Western Australia in 1991. Exploring the political influences of the "drama of rule" in the trilogy *English Public Schools and Ritualistic Imperialism* – *Elixir of Empire, Chains of Empire,* and *Rituals of Empire* – he applies the paradigm to a Middle Eastern setting in the quintet *Magicians of the Gulf.* Together the eight books comprise *The Ritocracy Octet.* The words *ritocracy, ritualocracy* and *epiphemera* are of his devising, as are a number of other terms appearing in a glossary in *Rituals of Empire* (Regency).

Tonbridge School Band, 1938. The School Arms are just discernable as decorations on the drums. The boars' heads refer to the arms of the school's founder, Sir Andrew Judde.

Elixir of Empire

The English Public Schools,
Ritualism, Freemasonry, and Imperialism

Second Edition
Volume One in the trilogy English Public
Schools and Ritualistic Imperialism

P. J. Rich

By degrees 'the public school spirit'
became one of the most potent
of the imperial elixirs.
—A. P. Thornton

Regency Press (London & New York) Ltd.
125 High Holborn, London WC1V 6QA

In memory of Otto Henry Miller, who gave an enthusiasm for books and history to his grandson.

Masonic Altar. Recalling a boy's curiosity about his grandfather's Masonic insignia.

CONTENTS

A terrified candidate begins his Masonic journey
and his introduction to the icons of rule.

ILLUSTRATIONS

The Heraldry Society in London.

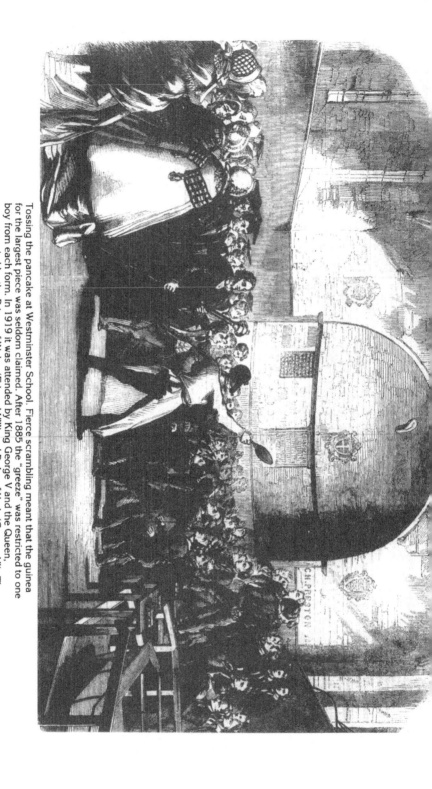

Tossing the pancake at Westminster School. Fierce scrambling meant that the guinea for the largest piece was seldom claimed. After 1885 the "greeze" was restricted to one boy from each form. In 1919 it was attended by King George V and the Queen, accompanied by the Prince of Wales (Edward VIII) and Duke of York (George VI). The ceremony was taken up elsewhere by schools seeking an authentic public school atmosphere, e.g. by Shawnigan Lake School in British Columbia.

FOREWORD

In the 1987 British elections, the English public schools were a major issue. High on the Labour Party's priority list, if or when it achieves power, is the fulfilment of pledges to abolish private education.

The connection between Imperialism and the public schools that Mr. Rich now substantiates has been acknowledged in passing only. Herbert Branston Gray, Headmaster of Bradfield, in *The Public Schools and Empire* (1913) was concerned that the public schools were not offering the right training for those destined to be leaders in the Empire. Other early public school publicists were H. H. Almond of Loretto, M. J. Rendall of Winchester and J. E. C. Welldon of Harrow. Sir Cyril Norwood, Headmaster of Harrow, in *The English Tradition of Education* (1929) included a final chapter which places the public schools on a macro- (or non-domestic) scale.

It is E. C. Mack, significantly an American and fellow countryman of Paul Rich, who could be acknowledged as the first *historian of education* to place the public schools in an Imperialist setting. In *Public Schools and British Opinion since 1860*, he devoted a chapter to this. His treatment was, however, conducted through an examination of writers such as Kipling and A. C. Benson.

Mr. Rich has written a book which is entirely concerned with the links between the British Empire and the English Public School and documents the connection between the schools and Imperial freemasonry. No other book, to my knowledge, has ventured in such areas. The late Meston

Harrow School. Heraldry embraces the ceremonial of officers of arms, while 'armoury' is a restrictive term concerning coats of arms. Victorian school magazines mention talks to the boys on both. Some schools had antiquarian societies which studied the subjects in considerable detail.

Batchelor's *Cradle of Empire* (1981) saw Temple Grove Preparatory School as a positive contributor to the Empire, but it was not about the Empire *per se*. Jonathan Gathorne-Hardy in *The Public School Phenomenon* (1977) claimed that his was *the* comprehensive book on the English Public School, but in the space of 457 pages he devoted three pages specifically to the Empire.

John R. de S. Honey in *Tom Brown's Universe*, despite the title, did not consider the topic. His 'Universe' did not extend to examining the role of English Public Schools in developing the Empire. Professor Honey presented the literature of the English Public School with a concept which has influenced later books of that genre, but his book must still be seen as one written in the older mould in which the British Empire is not a main concern.

Also typical of such past studies was Brian Simon's and Ian Bradley's *The Victorian Public School* (1975) which dealt with topics such as the public school novel; Thomas Arnold and other Victorian headmasters; the ideal of manliness; militarism; athleticism; football and the public school ethos, and school architecture. Whatever else it did, it did not examine the links between the English Public School and the British Empire. The old model was a domestic one concerned with institutions and personalities within the schools themselves.

J. A. Mangan's book on *Athleticism in the Victorian and Edwardian Public School* (1981), with its examination of the ideology of manliness and philathleticism, foreshadowed his sequel, *The Games Ethic and Imperialism* which was devoted to Athleticism in a variety of Imperialist settings. Meanwhile literature on the British Empire has been burgeoning for years, perhaps the most significant for students of the English Public School being Correlli Barnett's *The Collapse of British Power* (1972) in which the loss of the Empire was attributed to the failure of public schools to adapt. Edward Thring, in particular, was in my view wrongly arraigned for his share in the late nineteenth century 'softer' development of the English Public School. But that is another story.

Alleyn's School. Similarities to the Dulwich arms should be noted. Dulwich being the senior school on the foundation. See page 23.

Foreword

It is against this background that Paul Rich's book is to be warmly welcomed. His is an advance on much written previously and the first book which fully deals with ritualism, the British Empire and the public schools. He considers the cultural hegemony of the English Public School as a chief characteristic of the Empire. He establishes the close links between the two institutions and, in doing so, the value to public school boys of the 'talismans and totems' which comprise the symbols of public school ideology.

This study is largely concerned with the nineteenth century, but the final chapter gives a valuable assessment of the public school in post-Imperial days and notes how if in the Victorian era the schools were concerned with principles—enunciated by prophets such as Thring and Arnold—in the twentieth century they have embraced pragmatism in their endeavour to survive political threat. Mr. Rich is to be congratulated on this original analysis. It comes at a time when the Public School is again part of controversy. His suggestion about the internationalization of the schools is intriguing and deserves a wide audience.

Donald Leinster-Mackay
The University of Western Australia

Pinnock's Catechism of Heraldry. This important treatise influenced the nineteenth-century growth in heraldic interest.

ACKNOWLEDGEMENTS

This book was begun at The University of Western Australia in 1982. I would like to thank the University Library, and particularly Ms. Audrey Black, for many favours. I have benefited greatly by association with the Department of Education of the University and its members, including Associate Professor Ian Birch, Dr. Laadan Fletcher, and Dr. Clive Whitehead. The same can be said for the Western Australia Computing Centre staff, including Mr. Rob Van Zanten.

Over the years I have profited from the use of the India Office Library in London, and from the help of Ms. Penelope Tuson and Dr. Steven Ashton. Many hours have been spent in the Library of the United Grand Lodge of England, and there I have had the assistance of Mrs. J. H. Hall. Time has also passed happily in the Royal Commonwealth Society Library. I am grateful to its librarian, Mr. Donald Simpson.

I am especially grateful to the librarians of the Doha Club in Qatar, Mr. K. George and Mr. T. Jeyasothy. The Club's library has afforded an amiable setting for some animated discussions about schools around the world. Mr. Brian Devlin, Mr. Robert Jarman, and Dr. A. R. Kutrah have read parts of the manuscript for this book, but of course they are not responsible for the mistakes.

The greatest thanks go to Associate Professor Donald Leinster-Mackay, a distinguished historian of education. It was my good fortune to have met him at The University of Western Australia and to have had the opportunity to have his good natured admonishments.

I am at fault for any errors, and should *Elixir* give the impression that I am critical of the public schools and of British education, let me add that I am also an admirer.

P. J. Rich, Doha, Qatar, June, 1988.

The boys at Greyfriars repent their errors.

PREFACE

This is a book about a 'secret curriculum'. All educational establishments have goals that are quite outside their printed prospectuses. The English public schools certainly did. There is in fact no more successful example of how schools teach *outside* the classroom than that peculiar English contribution to education, which was not public in any accepted use of the word.

The public schools kept company with British Imperialism for as long as the Empire survived. They persisted after it died, and they remain a political issue in Britain. More and more, scholars are realizing that they are at the heart of any discussion of how the Empire worked.

We ignore the political and social effects of education at considerable peril. More than has been suspected, schools provide a nation's ideology. The connection between public schools and the Empire was a classic case of symbiosis.

The schools developed an elaborate system of totems and talismans. Their rituals were re-enacted all over the world. The rich symbolism of schooldays prepared colonial administrators for staging the Imperial drama. The British rulers recreated their adolescent triumphs, to the discomfort of their hapless subjects in Bahrain and Burma. The Imperial equivalent of school prize day was the occasional durbar when loyalty was rewarded with the Order of the Bath or the Star of India.

Moreover, the public schools became deeply involved with that other controversial affiliation of the English gentleman, freemasonry. There has been virtually no mention of just how

Freemasons' Hall, Georgetown, British Guyana.
Under foreign suns, sons of the Empire remembered that *Coelum Non Mutat Genus* meant "The Clime does not change the breed."

closely allied the two institutions were (and are).

When her possessions won independence, Britain was left with schools that were geared to meeting the needs of a now vanished global domain. The public school problem remained. In the last chapter, a proposal is made for how independent education might defuse the political threats to its existence.

Note to Second Edition, 1992.

The first edition in 1989 was intended as an introduction, with a series planned. *The Ritocracy Octet* includes a trilogy, *English Public Schools and Ritualistic Imperialism*, and a quintet, *Magicians of the Gulf.*

The trilogy's titles are *Elixir of Empire, Chains of Empire,* and *Rituals of Empire.* Its paradigm about ritualism is applied in the quintet to a specific situation in the Arabian Gulf. In 1991 *Chains of Empire* appeared and *Rituals of Empire* is forthcoming, all three published by Regency and benefiting enormously from the advice of John Thorpe.

A book in the *Magicians of the Gulf* quintet has already appeared. *The Invasions of the Gulf: Radicalism, Ritualism and the Shaikhs* (Allborough, Cambridge, 1991). Four more are projected: The *Raj in the Arabian Gulf, Creating the Arabian Gulf, The Gulf Oil Wars and Col. Lawrence's Ghost,* and *The Gulf, Zionism, and Billy Bunter.* Allborough also has published eight books edited by me relating to "Schoolboy Rulers of the Middle East", out-of-print titles about the region during and after World War I: *Iraq and Imperialism, A Soldier in Kurdistan, A Voyage into the Gulf, Wartime in Baghdad 1917, Chaos in Iraq, The Iraqi Mind, Arab War Lords and Iraqi Stargazers* and the penultimate *Iraqi, Iran, and Ritual Murder.* Those interested in the public schools and the Middle East may find them useful.

Heraldry, partly avataric and partly evocative, is "the business of the heralds", including marshaling great occasions and upholding the rôle of ceremony. In reviewing *Elixir of Empire* for the *Times Educational Supplement,* Dr. J.A. Mangan was taken by my point about heraldic consciousness and Freemasonry supporting the thesis about ritualocracy and Imperialism, which suggested that in this edition more illustrations of heraldry and Masonic symbolism would be appropriate.

Paul Rich,
The University of Western Australia,
November, 1992.

CHAPTER ONE

GRAMSCI AND
THE ENGLISH PUBLIC SCHOOL

*It was the sort of Look that kept the Empire
together, or quelled it at least. Armed with that
Look and perhaps a riding crop, white men could
keep order easily among the clubs and spears.*

William Golding, *The Pyramid*

If politicians understood how profound were the implications of schooling, schools might be meddled with even more
than they have been. To understand the British Empire, one
must understand the public school and its rituals. Indeed, to
comprehend fully British life, one must understand the public
schools.

The nineteenth century saw an expansion in these peculiar
institutions, which seized the opportunity to prepare boys for
service in an Empire embracing a quarter of the world.[1] Their
influence on Imperialism deserves more notice.[2] Rather than
being a result of its expansion, like the music hall songs and
biscuit boxes adorned with Union Jacks, public schools were
where its rituals were nurtured. Imperial administration
became in many ways an extension of public school life.

A startling similarity exists between the Empire and
the schools, especially in the way in which the two used
ritualism as an instrument of control.[3] Theirs was a
symbiotic relationship. As the Empire expanded, the schools

15

Viscount Hayashi Japanese Ambassador in 1904
when he was master of Empire Lodge in London
He played a part in the signing of the Anglo-
Japanese Alliance and became Japanese Foreign
Minister.

flourished.[4] The inter-dependence of the two means that explaining either, without looking at the way they reinforced each other, is unacceptable.

Lately a renewed interest has been expressed in determining the educational background of Imperial bureaucracies. The Oxford academic and ex-Sudanese and Nigerian civil servant, A. H. M. Kirk-Greene, has been at the forefront in calling for study of the schooling of the Imperial leadership.[5] But the relationship of education and Imperialism will not be left to political historians.

If that were so in the past, a reason was that educational history at the time was largely institutional history. However, the small group of public school historians have become aware of the wider relevance of their work. In particular, J. A. Mangan, a leading historian of Imperial education, has repeatedly emphasized the need for detailed examinations of the consequences of public school relationships.[6]

If any more proof of interest in the topic is necessary, in his magisterial book *Orientalism*, Edward Said makes a similar suggestion.[7] Said is himself the product of Victoria College, the 'Eton of Egypt'. More recently he has achieved considerable prominence as a possible mediator between the Palestinians and the United States and Israel, respected by all sides for the quality of his scholarship. His observations in particular should prompt investigation of the relationship between pedagogy and politics in the Empire, and the study of the ways that the public schools supported British ascendancy.

Cultural Hegemony

During an era when the West's dominance draws ever deeper resentment, Antonio Gramsci's ideas have been frequently invoked to describe the totality of Western influence. Political imperialism, as Gramsci recognized, was only the tip of the iceberg. If Western colonialism had solely relied on political structures, hostility would have faded long ago, but imperialism was far more ambitious.

16

Some Studies in Neckwear. Contemporary recognition of the comparative humour of school dress, from *The Boy's Own Book of School Yarns*.

Not surprisingly, Gramsci's work was invoked by Said,[8] who observed that cultural history was deficient without reference to Gramsci.[9] Gramsci's pertinence originates partly in his recognition of the subtleness of *hegemony* and of his recognition of the tacit consent of the under class to the mores of the prestigious dominant elite.[10] Imperialism's achievement was not in its *imposition*, but in its winning ready and lasting *acceptance* from the ruled. Its cultural hegemony was accepted long after its political side was denounced.

Although Marx claimed that the ruling class was also the ruling intellectual force,[11] it fell to Gramsci to see the full implications of such a statement.[12] The insight was not solely his,[13] but the eloquence of his tempestuous and tragic life has helped to link hegemony with his name. He provides a starting point for any examination of how schools influenced the British Empire.

Hegemonic forces à *la* Gramsci are not only crass class pressures or blatant social control. They also include the social rituals. In contrast with Marx's rude analysis, a Gramscian analysis has room for the small nuances, the court dances. Nowhere did such nuances flourish as fully as in the public schools.

With the importance of cultural hegemony more and more recognized, educational historians have come under notice that views previously accepted will *not* be sufficient when thoroughly examined.[14] It is no longer enough to study the declared curriculum: the secret curriculum is fully as important. The totems and taboos of school ritualism are as critical or more critical than the textbooks.

Almost all discussion of cultural hegemony along these lines is negative. Few if any have claimed that it was beneficial to those subjected to it. Third world partisans in particular portray the West as the 'Satan', castigating the brain-washing that starts in the cradle. Arthur Koestler wrote: "*Pro patria mori dulce et decorum est*, whichever the *patria* into which the stork happens to drop you."[15]

On the other hand, schools do need ritual and require some

17

Sprat and Harold overcome the villain.
Adventures transpired in proper school uniform.
From *Our Own Schoolboy's Annual.*

ceremonial. Yet today it must reflect the aspirations of a people, and not of their former colonial rulers. There is little doubt that the public school influence encouraged the growth of elitist education in the Empire, and the withering away of traditional schooling. Where some of the attitudes it encouraged have continued, so have some of the consequences.

Governing With Ritualism

Imperialism was frequently more reliant on ritual than on arms or money.[16] Imbued with public schoolism, the British governed with ritualism.[17] Their activities sometimes had little to do with overt political goals. This contradicts the view that socio-political rationalism provided an adequate description of motives and policies.[18]

In any case, political power sometimes served cultural hegemony rather than the reverse. There is a passion that comes with cultural causes. Some religious wars and some racial conflagrations can be summarized as political or economic, but certainly not all. The public school traditions that affected the Empire had emotional undertones that had little to do with geo-political considerations.[19]

The Empire required rituals, which old boys enthusiastically espoused. In school they had their prefectorial wands and hierarchy of colours, and in the Empire they instituted similar honours. Gramsci was fascinated by how such people used ritualism in rationalizing the irrational. No better example of this idea exists than the public schools and the British Empire, awash as they were in symbolism.

These rituals kept millions of people in their place.[20] To orchestrate them, the British Imperialists became impresarios, directing a great worldwide extravaganza. Their outward appearance changed dramatically as the Imperial pageant became more elaborate. This is shown by the contrast between the sloppy East India Company functionary

18

The Kaiser-i-Hind. Instituted by Queen Victoria, the award illustrated is from the reign of George V. Heraldry, honours, and hegemony were intimately connected.

Our Magistrate. From George Atkinson's series on Anglo-Indian life, *Curry & Rice.* Captain in the Bengal Engineers. Atkinson also wrote *Pictures from the North* and *The Campaign in India 1857-1858.* "Chutney", the magistrate shown directing the metalling of a road and receiving a petition, was replaced in the later nineteenth century by the sartorially-conscious Indian Political Service officers.

Lord Hardinge in the Robes of the Order of the Star of India Charles
Hardinge (1858-1944), enobled as Baron Hardings of Penshurst, was brother
of the third Viscount Hardinge. A Harrovian, he was Under-Secretary of State
for Foreign Affairs (1906-10 and 1916-20). As Viceroy of India (1910-16), he
Promoted British invasion of Iraq and was Grand Master of the Most
Exalted Order of the Star of India.

in the "Curry & Rice" print (See *Our Magistrate, page 19*) and the imperious Lord Hardinge dripping with decorations (See *Lord Hardinge in the Robes of the Order of the Star of India, page 20*).

Many of the traditions that the public schools were famous for were late Victorian inventions, reinforced by what have hitherto been the unexplored activities of numerous public school and colonial masonic lodges. This point will be expanded in subsequent chapters.

A current frontier of Imperial and educational history is in investigating how education influenced Imperial policy. If old boys exerted an influence through ritualism learned in school, more effort will assuredly uncover more evidence of how throughout their lives they relived their juvenile triumphs. Research will reveal how in distant outposts they recreated their school experiences. The conviction of this book is that this will prove the case.

Lifelong Ways of Thinking

The Empire was not run by a large group: the famous Indian Civil Service had about 1,000 active officers. Each individual counted, which is why it is especially noteworthy that public school influence on individuals went far beyond the 'Sloane Ranger' advantage of having attended prestigious institutions.[21] Schoolboy loyalties were not left behind when a boy left the sixth form. The school inculcated lifelong ways of thinking and acting.[22]

It will be granted that school mannerisms have been extensively ridiculed and viewed with bemusement. The Wall Game at Eton seems more folklore than leadership training, belonging in the same category with Morris Dancers and swan clipping on the Thames. But public school ritualism was taken extremely seriously, and although the customs were curious, the respect for ritual was carried into manhood. The

School experiences had enduring consequences.

attitudes absorbed at school became immensely influential because the Empire was almost entirely run by old boys.[23]

Which public schools they attended is *not* as central an issue as the fact that almost all the Imperial hierarchy attended public schools. The status of individual public schools has provoked indeterminable argument.[24] Pretentious upstarts encountered formidable resistance. Headmasters' Conference membership did not serve as an infallible guide. One authority, in despair over any definition, suggested that a public school was any school "like Rugby". The debate over this sort of issue has at times obscured the fact that public schools were by and large more alike than they were different.

Causality

Whether fifty or one hundred or two hundred schools are included in the magic circle, the observation stands that the schools Imperial influence was in inverse proportion to the numbers of students enrolled.[25] The wonder is how few schools' there were in comparison to their consequences for society.

The influence of the schools did not come about accidentally. Imperialism was part of the curriculum rather than an incidental.[26] Everywhere in the Empire the consequences of this could be observed. In such remote places as the Arabian Gulf, the old boys held sway, causing one authority to remark: "In the final analysis, without such men Britain could never have taken a strong Gulf position in the 1890s and, despite, or perhaps because of, every challenge emerged in 1914 with one which was all the stronger."[27]

Finding a colony, protectorate, or indeed a stray acre of the Empire that was not exposed to public school virtues and vices approaches the impossible. It is doubly impressive to see the influence on regions such as the Middle East, where despite the environment's hostility the British nevertheless managed to knot the old school tie firmly.

22

Sign on the lodge building in Victoria, Seychelles.

Putting Away Childish Things

Non-Englishmen have found it bizarre that schooldays influenced such distant lands in a degree comparable to or exceeding that of military or economic influence. Decisions were supposed to be made rationally, based on reports and careful analysis, and not on memories of house matches and tuck shops. Still, many decisions of the British in the Empire were 'fire brigade' responses to crises. The decision-making process was often spur-of-the-moment.[28]

For this and other reasons, Imperial administrators drew heavily on their school backgrounds.[29] If such a claim is hard to accept, one reason for scepticism is that admitting to the lifelong influence of a few years in school requires acknowledging the power of happenstance,[30] and goes against one's feeling about people behaving logically. The issue of public school influence is also one that has inflamed emotions about equality and inequality. Convictions about free-will resist such juvenile determinism.

With the writer of Ecclesiastes, the observer of these sometimes peculiar totems and taboos feels that men should put away childish things. Nevertheless, public schools instilled a 'language of life'. If the school years were full of plaudits and trophies, the adult years sought to recreate those triumphs.[31] If the schooldays were ignominious, the adult years were spent in attempts to lay the ghosts of humiliation to rest.

Viewing with animosity the extreme devotion of old boys to their schools, adversaries have often gleefully but prematurely announced the schools' demise. The Labour Party has put their eradication in the same category as nuclear weapons. A writer in the *Times Educational Supplement* complained: ". . . And to the uninitiated, the whole picture is more than a little repellent: even when approached in the spirit of impartial social anthropology, it is hard to study it with detachment."[32]

One reply to such criticism has been that the old boys exemplified the best of the English character. In fact, the

Saint Michael's University School, Victoria, British Columbia. Incorporating University School's 1906 arms, and St.Michael's 1910 arms with stars from the Dulwich College arms, as its founder was a Dulwich old boy. (See page 10).

privilege of wearing the old school tie has been made out as requiring an uncommon altruism because it exacted such sacrifices to duty. Although this has met with incredulity, possibly the cynicism with which public school virtuousness was greeted went too far.[33] Not all the Empire's noble moments were faked.

Even so, it is quite understandable that those who did not go to public school, and have had to confront life without its advantages, are vitriolic about the unfairness. The issue remains a highly charged one, and the animosities are kept alive by the way that the schools have stubbornly remained a force.

The problem, in fact, has never been confined to England. In Australia and Canada there have been questions about having schools which perpetuate loyalties that many want put aside as affectations in the same category as Imperial honours and Privy Council appeal, Imperial vestiges to be eliminated on the road to republicanism.

So the public schools are one of education's contentious issues. An article in the *Guardian* under the title "Bunter and the Boys Who Can't Grow Up" seethed: "Does it matter that a large section of what passes for the intelligentsia in this Philistine country is stuck with the mentality of the *Gem*, the *Magnet*, *Boys' Own Paper*, the tuck shop and six of the best? I cheerfully take the risk of being called portentous (and probably much worse) when I say that I think it does."[34]

A Fraternity

The schools set an elite apart by ceremonies not unlike those of a masonic lodge. Indeed, frequently there crop up references to the freemasonry of the schools, using the word in the broad sense of brotherhood. But this idea of the old boys as a fraternity set apart by rituals was carried a step further, because the actual society of freemasons had many ties with the schools. Public school freemasonry was a flourishing empire of its own.[35]

24

Order of the Secret Monitor. Also known as the Order of David and Jonathan, this Masonic society was active in India, with conclaves established in Madras and Calcutta in 1889.

In summary, school rituals may initially appear to be trivial, but they were fundamental in preparing boys for Imperial responsibility. They contributed to the faith in the public school boy's ability to exercise leadership. This ability was widespread and widely admired, sometimes by the native peoples that were its victims. Brian Devlin, a longtime teacher in Qatar in the Arabian Gulf, wrote: "Arabs are remarkably attracted to 'presence' and the public school old boys possessed this kind of *presence* that characterized the sheikhs of Arabia."[36]

The schools were more central to the making of the Empire than has been acknowledged, showing boys how to rule by ritual. In *Tom Brown's Schooldays*, Mrs. Arnold said of Rugby old boys, "Many is the brave heart now doing its work and bearing its load under the Indian sun and in Australian farms and clearings." *Pari passu*, this was true of the British Empire as a whole.

The Rugby and Dr.Arnold of Thomas Hughes'
novel had more influence on education than did
the real school and headmaster.

NOTES — CHAPTER ONE

1. Donald Leinster-Mackay, *The Rise of the English Prep School*, The Falmer Press, London and Philadelphia, 1984, 154. Unless specified, books were published in London.

2. See Ian Hansen, *By Their Deeds: A Centenary History of Camberwell Grammar School, 1886-1986*, Camberwell Grammar School, Canterbury (Victoria), 1986, 298.

3. See Ralph Braibanti, *Asian Bureaucratic Systems Emergent from the British Imperial Tradition*, Duke University Press, Durham, North Carolina, 1966, 21. Also Bernard S. Cohn, *Recruitment and Training of British Civil Servants in India, 1600-1860, Ibid.*, 87-141.

4. See Derek Verschoyle, *Indian Innocence, Ltd.* in Graham Greene, ed., *The Old School: Essays by Divers Hands*, Jonathan Cape, 1934, 200.

5. A. H. M. Kirk-Greene, review of *The British in the Sudan, 1898-1956* by Robert O'Collins and Francis M. Deng, *Journal of Imperial & Commonwealth History*, Vol. XIV, No. 2, January 1986, 128.

6. ". . . it is generally accepted that public schoolboys ruled the British Empire, but our knowledge has not yet proceeded much beyond this generalization." J. A. Mangan, *The Games Ethic and Imperialism*, Viking, Harmondsworth, 1986, 75.

Canadian Heraldry Authority. Now supplanting the College of Heralds in London, it gives Canadians their own source of ritualistic expertise.

7. Edward W. Said, *Orientalism*, Routledge & Kegan Paul, 1978, 24.

8. *Ibid*, 6-7, 11, 14, 25-26.

9. " . . . certain cultural forms predominate over others, just as certain ideas are more influential than others; the form of this cultural leadership is what Gramsci has identified as *hegemony*, an indispensable concept for any understanding of cultural life in the industrial West." *Ibid*, 6-7.

10. Antonio Gramsci, *Selections from the Prison Notebooks*, qtd. T. J. Jackson Lears, "The Concept of Cultural Hegemony: Problems and Possibilities", *American Historical Review*, Vol. 90, No. 3, June 1985, 568.

11. Considering that Marx and Engels liked the pleasures of the table, and that Marx fought a duel and Engels fenced, one wonders if they would have proceeded further down the road of the English gentleman and, had they had sons, sent them to a public school.

12. Ted Tapper and Brian Salter, *Education and the Political Order: Changing Patterns of Class Control*, Macmillan, 1978, 56.

13. See Rudolf von Albertini, *European Colonial Rule, 1880-1940: The Impact of the West on India, Southeast Asia, and Africa*, Clio Press, Oxford, 1982, xix-xxvi.

14. Thomas Nemeth, *Gramsci's Philosophy*, Harvester Press, Brighton, 1980, 133.

15. Arthur Koestler, *Janus: A summing up*, Picador, 1983, 13-14.

16. Lears, "The Concept of Cultural Hegemony", *American Historical Review*, 572.

Military Order of the Foreign Wars. A decoration given by an American organization: in the absence of official orders and heraldic authorities, Americans have a bevy of voluntary groups that confer distinctions.

17. Tapper and Salter, *Educational and the Political Order*, 57.

18. *Ibid.*, x.

19. A. P. Thornton, *The Imperial Idea and Its Enemies*, Second Edition, Macmillan, 1985, 92. See Joseph V. Gemia, *Gramsci's Political Thought*, Oxford University Press, 1981. Walter L. Adamson, *Hegemony and Revolution: A Study of Antonio Gramsci's Political and Cultural Theory*, University of California, Berkeley, 1981.

20. "There was symbolic inculcation not only of loyalty but also of obeisance." J. A. Mangan, *Athleticism in the Victorian and Edwardian Public School*, Cambridge University Press, Cambridge, 1981, 161.

21. "Of course a hunting family's son is sent to one of the five schools with its own beagle pack: Eton, Ampleforth, Marlborough, Radley or Stowe." Ann Barr & Peter York, *The Official Sloane Ranger Diary*, Ebury Press, London, 1983, 107.

22. This applies equally to those natives in the Empire who went to public schools. The phenomenon of Western sponsored elites is receiving increased academic notice. See Ira William Zartman, ed., *Elites in the Middle East*, Praeger, New York, 1980.

23. ". . . the attempt to demonstrate that successful candidates for entry to elites were mostly educated at schools which are then treated as elite schools obscures the extent to which the schools themselves acted as agencies for recruitment to the more privileged classes from the less privileged." J. R. de S. Honey, *Tom Brown's Universe: The Development of the Victorian Public School*, Millington, 1977, 289.

24. Besides Honey's approach in *Tom Brown's Universe, Ibid.*, which employed games' fixtures to evaluate the social status of

28

Stowe School. Stowe's arms represent its first four boarding houses. Such houses often have their own arms.

schools, one could use membership in the Freemasons' Public Schools' Lodge Council, admissions to the Public Schools' Club in London, the appearance of a school's notices in *The Times*, and numerous other criteria.

25. Alfred B. Badger, *The Public Schools and The Nation*, Robert Hale, 1944, 21.

26. T. W. Bamford, *Rise of the Public Schools: a study of boys' public schools in England and Wales from 1837 to the present day*, Nelson, 1967, 240-41.

27. Briton Cooper Busch, *Britain and the Persian Gulf, 1894 - 1914*, University of California Press, Berkeley, 1967, 388.

28. Edmund King, the historically-orientated comparative educationist, wrote: "*Decision* depends upon the state of public opinion, the state of socio-economic readiness and development, perhaps even on external example, an international shock, or indeed an accident." Edmund J. King, *Other Schools and Ours: comparative studies for today*, Fifth Edition, Holt, Rinehart and Winston, 1979, 60.

29. *Ibid.*

30. *Ibid.*, 46.

31. *Ibid.*, 45.

32. Roy Foster, "Oh, Jolly Good!", *Times Educational Supplement*, 22 November 1985, 25.

33. Mangan, *Athleticism*, 205.

34. Richard Boston, "Bunter and the Boys Who Can't Grow Up", *Guardian*, London, 5 September 1985, 10.

35. See the author's article "Public School Freemasonry and

University Lodge, Toronto. This University of Toronto Lodge has associations as well with Upper Canada College and other boarding schools.

the Empire" in J. A. Mangan, ed., *Benefits Bestowed*, Manchester University Press, 1988.

36. Brian Devlin to Paul Rich, 2 May 1986.

Etonians shop for flowers. All went well as long as the underclass, whether at home or in the Empire, knew its place and maintained a deferential good humour.

CHAPTER TWO

LINKS NOT EASILY SEVERED

*If it were possible to give these boys a solid
education in their language and in ours, the
influence for good they may exercise on the next
generation is beyond calculation, by it we should
instruct them in our system, and attach them by a
link which would not be easily severed.*
            W. M. Coghlan, Political Resident, Aden,
      in founding the predecessor of Aden College, 1856.

"By degrees 'the public school spirit'", remarked A. P.
Thornton, "became one of the most potent of the imperial
elixirs."[1] As the Empire grew, the schools did as well, adding
playing fields, boarding houses, and prestige. New schools
opened which, as James Morris aptly put it, ". . . lay
somewhere near the heart of the imperial ethic."[2]

The cultural hegemony achieved over freshly acquired
possessions, proved as important as any force used in their
acquisition.[3] What sustained this hegemony was a ritualism
which may have counted for more in the end than military
might.[4] This hegemonic and cultural view of Imperialism
modifies the stock explanations that have identified it with
financial self-interest.[5]

However, it is not an entirely new perspective. While it was
generally taken for granted that public schools provided the
Empire's leaders, Herbert Gray (Headmaster of Bradfield
1880-1910) anticipated the later discussion of the con-

31

Bradfield College. The school had no proper coat
until 1924 when old boys paid for a grant. The
overweight falcons come from the founder's arms.

sequences in *The Public Schools and the Empire*[6] (1913). Although his chief interest was in the schools doing a better job in preparing boys for their Imperial careers, he was aware of the ideological implications.

Perhaps it is time to take up the discussion where Gray left off. For educators in former British colonies, the issue is not only an historical one. The schools' influence did not completely fade away when the Empire did. Like a pensioned colonel eking out his retirement in a seaside resort, public schoolism persisted. Moreover, like those colonels who when they retired stayed abroad, the elitist educational tradition persisted overseas.[7]

Tampering With History

Few subjects in educational history have been more subject to historical distortion. E. W. Hornung satirizes one such misrepresentation in his story "The Field of Philippi", drawing liberally on the history of Uppingham School where he was a pupil during its transformation by Thring. A wealthy old boy is asked, but refuses, to pay for a statue of his school's founder:

> Why spend money on a man who had been dead two hundred years? What good could it do him or the school? Besides, he was only technically our founder. He had not founded a great public school. He had founded a little country grammar school which had pottered along for a century and a half. The great public school was the growth of the last fifty years, and no credit to the pillar of piety.[8]

This 'second founding' is exactly what did happen to many schools. They benefited from a fortuitous alliance that was

32

Royal Order of Scotland. Senior Grand Warden's jewel – this worldwide Masonic body became well established in India. Its curious ritual is almost entirely in rhyme.

The Visit of the Prince of Wales to India. The Procession in Bombay, 1875. There was grumbling in Parliament about the expense of the trip, which at the time was the most ambitious royal tour ever attempted, but it was a great success. Highlights included elephant wrestling, the Taj Mahal (inevitably), and a durbar for native princes when Edward conferred decorations while seated on a solid silver throne. See page 140-141.

Doon School Pageant, 1937. Heraldic elephants are neither infrequent nor recent, appearing as early as the time of the Crusades. However, the castle seems derived from the Indian howdah (right).See page 148.

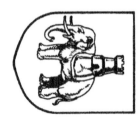

struck with the upper and middle classes and themselves
during the nineteenth century.[9] The social embarrassment of
the schools' origins, which often were as foundations for the
poor, were speedily supplanted by a bogus history. As
Hornung suggests, the minor versions of William of Wykeham
who started schools out of piety were displaced by less
attractive patrons, the "Chinese" Gordons and industrial
tycoons.[10]

With their new outlook, the schools set about inventing a
good deal of ritual and familiarizing boys with the use of it as
a means of social control. The medals and uniforms of the
Empire reflected schooldays, and *vice versa*. The spectacle of
the royal visits around the world (see *Visit of the Prince of
Wales to India*, page 33) was matched by some of the
schools' ceremonials (see *Doon School Pageant*, page 34),
which in India on occasion used live camels and elephants.

The schools proved useful not only to the British, but to the
native ruling classes. The large number of overseas schools
founded in the nineteenth century demonstrates how readily
the local worthies took their lead from England. Third World
leaders would be quick to deny it, but analysis of the effects
of pre-independence agitation sometimes reveals that the
objections were not directed at Western institutions but at the
slowness with which they were introduced.[11]

The Convenient Partnership

The expansion of the schools was warmly supported by
those who did the recruiting for the Empire. On the other
hand, the door to Imperial service was closed to the boys of
any school that failed to practise the prescribed rites. The
schools were seized upon as an appropriate initiation for
Imperial careers.[12] Headmasters were forthcoming about
these new associations with the Empire. None of the
embarrassment existed over such connections that would be

Westminster School. An old boy was G.A.Henty,
whose stories of plucky lads braving all for the
Empire enthralled generations of readers.

felt today about such jingoism.

Much later, as British attitudes did change, the schools created social service corps as an option to their cadet corps. Boys began to visit the elderly or plant trees as an alternative to military drill. The decline of the cadet corps seemed to indicate a decline in the partnership between the schools and patriotism. A Royal Air Force officer complained to the Bedford School magazine:

> I am very surprised that you allowed the school magazine to publish a brief but scurrilous side-swipe at the Combined Cadet Force . . . the authors defined boys who chose the CCF as 'those who wanted to learn to kill'. This was a very cheap, ill-informed snipe.[13]

Any such doubts were far in the future when, in the years after the Clarendon Commission Report in 1864 on leading schools, the schools began turning out what Philip Mason and others have called 'The Guardians'. The choice of a Platonic term for the Imperial bureaucrats is quite apt, because the schools did emphasize notions of Platonic stewardship. These tenets permeated the Empire's consciousness. Plato's classes of guardians, warriors, and workers, were a reasonable idea to the Victorians.[14]

The guardians had no particular expertise, but that was made out to be an advantage, and they were equipped instead with a much admired panache identified with the schools.[15] The schools successfully produced an old boy Samurai, armed with an almost religious conviction of superiority.[16] The notion of an unplanned Empire supported the argument for these amateurs over the crude technocrats. Deprecation of expertise went with being a true public school product.

36

Queen's College, Taunton. A "homemade" coat with castle representing the borough of Taunton, escallops for Wesley because the school had Methodist origins, and Tudor rose for links with the University of London.

Links Not Easily Severed

"Provision Should Be Made"

Despite this veneration of studied inability, considerable prescience went into shaping the final product. As will be seen, much energy was expended in producing old boys. A procession of visiting speakers reminded them while they were in school of their destiny. There was little criticism of the effects of this system. The schools were a fixture that was accepted like the Monarchy and country houses or indeed ". . . like the Churches; it is impossible to criticize them at all without giving deep offence."[17]

Furthermore, Victorian schoolmasters likened the Empire favourably with the empires of antiquity.[18] Along with this analogy went the exhilarating thought that the new Rome required schools. When the British captured control of countries where the educational system had not been elitist, they were not deterred from creating schools that resembled the ones they had attended.[19]

Education was a political tool, and there was no ashamed reticence about the fact. It had the sanction of officialdom. In 1941, when there was a debate about establishing a school on the island of Bahrain for the sons of Arabian sheikhs, C. A. F. Dundas, the British Council Representative in the Near East, wrote in the strongest terms to Charles Prior, the British Political Resident for the Gulf, to dismiss a proposal for examinations in Bahrain:

> The principle of admission to the Kuliya (senior school) by competitive examination only would mean that the sons of Sheikhs and other notables would not necessarily be able to obtain any education after the age of 13 plus. I am convinced that provision should be made for them to receive further schooling . . .[20]

Dundas roundly criticized the idea of access to secondary education based on merit. Examinations would admit poor boys who should *not* be getting a secondary education, and

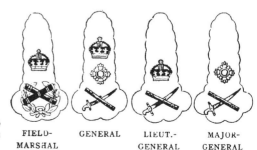

Royal Army Badges. From the chapter on patriotism in Lord Baden-Powell's *Scouting for Boys.* The Scouts enabled working class boys to appreciate some of the ritualism associated with public schools.

FIELD-MARSHAL   GENERAL   LIEUT.-GENERAL   MAJOR-GENERAL

exclude the sons of the powerful. This belief in a different education for each class, and of no education for the masses, was rooted in the public schools. The best facilities were for the future leaders, and the leavings were for the rest.

Bahrain was hardly the only place where such attitudes prevailed. The old boys were everywhere, partly as a consequence of the Empire-awareness of their schoolmasters.[21] The schools were Imperial employment agencies.[22]

Understandably, therefore, schooldays for a boy who had any doubts about the value of Imperialism could be highly unpleasant. The suicide of a Haileybury boy who had dared to question British intervention in Crete the very month of Queen Victoria's Diamond Jubilee celebration in June 1897, elicited no compassion from the *Illustrated London News*. Rather than deploring his death, it was the lad's anti-imperial sentiments that the *News* found bizarre: "It is probable that his mind was unhinged." [23]

If the popular literature of the day gives any indication, schooldays were full of dreams about honours to be won in distant lands. In this fertile pubescent soil, adolescents fantasized about their governorships. Around them, the chapel memorials, oil portraits, and the names of boarding houses reminded them of their right to Imperial preferment.[24] Pulp magazines and potboiler novels helped as well.

Old Boys in Arabia

Of course, the Empire encompassed extremes, and the public school influence varied greatly and unexpectedly. In the Middle East, for example, Imperialism and school elitism came together in some particularly surprising conjunctions. A peculiar literature compared school with Arabia—eccentric as this juxtaposition of green cricket pitches and shifting sands seems.[25] Recollections of schooldays led to highblown comparisons of bedouin life to school life.

The resemblances of Clifton to Kuwait are few, but that there was a fancied similarity is not so extraordinary as it

38

Joseph Lancaster Lodge. For Masons connected with London's Borough Road and Bangor Training Colleges, it was named for the educationist who popularised the monitorial system. Thus Masonry was extended to the state system.

seems. The golden days of the administrator's life had been at school. The feelings of an affinity between the Empire and the schools prompted a veteran of the Gulf and North-West Frontier to compare his postings with Winchester, and another to write from Arabia that Clifton was *his* Mecca.[26] Others claimed that Arab social organization paralleled that of the English schools.[27] Possibly examples could be found of the sun-stroked in other parts of the Empire who saw resemblances between Madras and Marlborough.

Imperial Headmasters

If British administrators talked about their satraps in school terms, the favour was returned as schools adopted an Imperial phraseology when describing their own history. Charles Whittaker's headmastership at Taunton School earned a tribute as if he were a brigadier planting the flag: ". . . he has extended the territory, making it a sort of British Empire in the way it has annexed things adjoining."[28]

The schools not only acquired an Imperial phraseology, but overseas 'ranches' where the Empire could be experienced at first hand and inner city 'missions' where the lower classes could be exorted to do their duty. Preparatory schools were spawned as feeders to maintain enrolments, as junior departments of public schools and as the creation of ambitious assistant masters and old boys who set up shop on their own. Thus empires were created by headmasters that matched the achievements of those entrepreneurs who added Fiji and Fujairah to the Imperial holdings.

Maintaining Kitibwa

The umbilical cord with England was a strong one.[29] The Indian Public Schools Society, an embryonic Woodard-style St. Nicholas Society, debated whether heads should come

39

Gibraltar Freemasonry. Device commemorating the 1989 visit of HRH The Duke of Kent for the 200th anniversary of Royal Lodge of Friendship.

from India, concluding that "previous experience in India would be rather a *disqualification*."[30]

Staff recruitment from England was not resented but demanded. At King's College Budo in Uganda, a locally appointed head had to suspend classes after the students assembled on the lawn with a blackboard calling for his resignation. A teacher sympathized: "Budo had grown used to having its headmasters specially imported from 'oversea' . . . To have a headmaster who had often visited the school as an assistant master from a neighbouring—and naturally, in the opinion of every Budo boy, an inferior—school, was a blow to Budo *kitibwa* (pride)."[31]

Percy Henn

Appointment of men to colonial headmasterships who had English school backgrounds was therefore a meaningful influence on Imperial education. An account of such a career, Percy Henn's, is appropriate and not untypical.

His father had been associated with the famous Prince Lee both as a boy and teacher at King Edward VI School, Birmingham, but sent Henn in 1873 to Christ's Hospital. Henn's own son and biographer, Wilfrid Henn, wrote: "Father's life for the next ten years was centred around this School of some six or seven hundred boys, for only twice a year, at Christmas and at Midsummer, did they go home for holidays. So home became little more than a 'hostel' in which they spent their holidays . . ..[32]

The school had a permanent influence on Henn, who became an active president of the Amicable Society of Blues and was invited back to preach at chapel. He wrote a sonnet expressing his love for the school.[33] With such feelings, not surprisingly he decided on education as a career and became second master at Hurstpierpoint. There he acquired an enthusiasm for Nathaniel Woodard's work. Wilfred Henn commented: ". . . he modelled his later work at Guildford on Woodard's ideals and principles . . ..[34]

40

Guildford Grammar School. Long a choice of prominent rural families in Western Australia, it is perhaps the school in Perth most resembling an English Public school.

After seven years at Hurstpierpoint, Henn became the founding headmaster of another Woodard foundation, Worksop. From Worksop he went to a parish in Western Australia, followed by a spell in England working for the Society for the Propagation of the Gospel. Finally, in 1909, came his great opportunity, an invitation to return to Western Australia as head of Guildford. Although it was established in 1896, Guildford Grammar School came into its own under Henn. He made it into a leading Australian institution.

Although he never realized hopes of a Woodard corporation that would found schools throughout Australia, his position at Guildford gave him great influence over the development of Australian education. The English public school continued to be his ideal, and when he died at 90 in 1961, he left bequests to Guildford and to the Amicable Society of Old Blues. His ashes were placed beneath the floor in Guildford School Chapel.[35] Thus, like the interment of Arnold in Rugby Chapel, Percival in Clifton's, or Sanderson in Oundle's, his remains consecrated his work.

Headmasters such as Henn were instrumental in the extension of school influence. Another of many examples was A. G. Fraser, who helped launch three schools: King's College Budo in Uganda, Trinity College Kandy in Sri Lanka, and Achimota College, Gold Coast.[36] If the overseas schools never quite turned out old boys in the English model, it was not for lack of trying.

Why Not the Original?

The British established overseas schools but seldom attended them, going back instead back to England. As a consequence, the natives suspected they were inferior. The Maharajah of Dhrangadhara indicated this feeling:

In 1935 the entire Palace School—minus the girls— was shipped off to England and an establishment was set up at a place called Millfield in Somerset. I

41

The University of Western Australia. Black swans are ubiquitous in Western Australian school and collegiate heraldry.

myself was soon packed off elsewhere—first to a prep school, where there was a lot of ragging, and then on to Haileybury, on the theory that 'since the Indian public schools were imitations of the schools in England, why go to an imitation and not the original?'[37]

Perhaps overseas public schools had less racial harassment than the Maharajah encountered, and they were an option for some upper class local families. Nathaniel Woodard had envisaged a College of Missionaries attached to Hurstpierpoint that would send men out into the Empire establishing schools.[38] The closest he came was in 1850 when he started a school for those who wanted to enter the service of the East India Company, but it was one of Woodard's few failures. It had closed by 1858.[39] Had Woodard's powers of salesmanship been turned loose on the Empire, the consequences could have been intriguing. He had the ability to have made the public school the dominant educational force in the Dominions.

Boys from the colonies were never unusual in English schools. The king of the Ashanti's son, Kofi Nti (known as 'Coffee') went to Cranleigh around 1880.[40] Probably many encountered the 'ragging' that the Maharajah of Dhrangadhara mentions. Walter Rhoades' school novel, *The Boy from Cuba* began:

"... What's the chap's name?"
"I don't know. Sambo, I suppose. If it isn't, it ought to be. Oh, it's a sickening business."
"... Why doesn't he go to a native school, with the other blackamoors?"[41]

As for the British, the sending of children back to England at the age of seven or eight was a fact of Imperial life.[42] This did not however deter the establishment of a network of schools in the colonies, struggling mightily to emulate those in England. The founding of these schools accelerated in the later nineteenth century, but the beginnings of overseas

42

Toronto Masonic Hall, 1884. That year there were an estimated 4000 Freemasons in the city.

English-style education were even earlier, if some rather free-wheeling colleges are taken into account.[43] These early schools were not public in the Arnoldian sense, any more than unreformed foundations at the same time in England were, but such efforts are significant because they show that the institutions overseas existed early enough to be influenced by the same social changes that public schools in England went through.

In particular, there were many schools started in India. Some of them eschewed the Spartan living conditions of their English peers. Mayo College at Ajmer, founded in 1873, had a rule that no student could have more than *three* personal servants, but the Maharajah of Kotah arrived with 200 whilst the Maharajah of Alwar arrived as a new boy with twenty polo ponies and eight carriage horses. The Indian public school historian R. P. Singh sceptically commented: "They were supposed to be offered education on the public schools' lines."[44]

As the remark implies, the legitimacy of colonial schools depended on faithfulness to the originals. Departures from the English pattern were suspect.[45] While the British were not the only colonial powers that had schools that imitated the ones at home,[46] they put extreme emphasis on exact replication. This included the rituals as well as the curriculum.[47]

The rituals were copied more conscientiously than the grammar lessons. The houses at King's in Uganda are a case in point:

> In 1906 only one dormitory had been ready for occupation and it was immediately christened 'England'. No one seems to know why. The second was finished by the end of the year and was called, just as mysteriously 'Turkey'. The beginnings of the English public school 'house spirit' were quickly established and when the third dormitory was built at the end of 1907 the boys who were to live in it decided that it was to be 'South Africa',

Sir Humphry Davy Lodge. Consecrated in Mount's Bay School Penzance, the lodge uses miners' safety lamps rather than candles.

after what they considered to be Britain's most important possession. The fourth, when finished, was to become 'Australia'. All this made the boys of 'Turkey' house feel distinctly unimperial and inferior.[48]

The Budo affair had a happy ending: 'Turkey' was renamed 'Canada'.

By thus copying the ritualism, the overseas schools hoped to produce real public school old boys, albeit swarthy with unpronounceable names.[49] The first headmaster of Budo, Henry Weatherhead, wrote to his successor, D. G. Herbert: "You know the one thing that sticks out in the memory of our talks with you is what you told us of the reality of the Budo spirit, which struck you so much on your arrival from Achimota, and seems as strong and potent in influence today 'forty years on'—as the Harrow song puts it."[50]

Budo affords a good example of how a school can become as significant in the establishment of its own country as Eton or Harrow were to England. In 1914 it hosted the coronation of the Kabaka of Buganda, His Highness Daudi Chwa II, in the school chapel.[51] The influence of such establishments on Imperialism has been neglected, partly because of the view that British educational policy overseas was largely one of benign neglect and missionary control. This in turn produced studies of overseas education that were anthropological or denominational rather than historical in emphasis.

Consequently, the public schools that were established throughout the Empire have been largely ignored. There were many. The roll covers all parts of the world: Victoria College in Alexandria, Harrison College in Barbados, Peterhouse in Zimbabwe, Timaru in New Zealand, the great schools of Australia such as St. Peter's Adelaide, Geelong Grammar, King's School Parramatta, and Melbourne Grammar School, to mention but a few. Cold showers and chapel proved exportable.

Schools achieved a reputation in their own countries scarcely less prestigious than that achieved by the English

44

Round Table Lodge of Mark Master Masons, Derbyshire. The phenomenon of service clubs has been accommodated by establishing lodges for club leaders, just as the growth of public schools led to establishment of school lodges.

public schools.[52] Upper Canada College was considered Canada's Eton, but nearly as important were Lower Canada College and Bishop's College in Quebec; St. Andrew's College and Ridley College of Ontario; St. George's and Shawnigan Lake schools in British Columbia. A cross-fertilization went on because overseas schools such as the Canadian ones were not limited in enrolment to youths of their own country. They had boys from other parts of the Empire.[53] The overseas schools proved as eclectic in their student bodies as their English counterparts, and through the years they continued so.[54] The coming together of students from different parts of the Empire in such schools offers a so far unresearched explanation for the spread of Imperial ideas.

Wherever they were located, what gave these schools a similarity was their skilful use of ritual. A visitor to St. Paul's, a New England boarding school cast in the English pattern, discerned the same totemism which formed the basis of the public school genius elsewhere:

> Oak panels engraved with the names of every graduate adorn the dining hall walls. Memorial Hall honours "old boys" who served in the two World Wars. Portraits of past rectors and beloved teachers look down on passers-by in almost every building on campus. In short, history and tradition intrude at every turning, their message crystal clear.[55]

Examples of schools espousing such totems can be offered *ad infinitum*. The schools' social standing was a tribute to how effective this could be in creating an elite. For example, in Jamaica the cachet imparted by Munro College, Wolmers, and Jamaica College blazers was a passport to high status.[56]

Before poking too much fun at such sartorial nuances, a comment should be recalled about the British part in introducing public schools to Uganda: "They paid Uganda the compliment of bringing it the best they knew".[57] Public school ritualism was a vigorous and energetic force in the Empire. The next chapter treats more fully its nuances.

45

King's School, Parramatta. Arguably Australia's oldest public school, King's is one of the most prominent. See Page 147.

NOTES—CHAPTER TWO

1. A. P. Thornton, *The Imperial Idea and Its Enemies: A Study in British Power,* St. Martin's Press, New York, 1966, 90.

2. James Morris, *Pax Britannica: The Climax of an Empire,* Penguin Books, Harmondsworth, 1984, 220.

3. It is hard to see how one could have taken place without the other. They were dependent on each other. The vitality of Victorian culture owed much to the Empire.

4. "Imperialism generally involves the collision of two or more cultures and a subsequent relationship of unequal exchange between or among them. What confuses the issues has been the inability of men to analyze their real motives for territorial or cultural expansion and to separate them from rationalizations devised after the fact." George H. Nadel and Perry Curtis, "Introduction", George H. Nadel and Perry Curtis, eds., *Imperialism and Colonialism,* Macmillan, 1964, 1.

5. See D. K. Fieldhouse, "Hobson and Economic Imperialism Reconsidered", Robin W. Winks, ed., *British Imperialism: Gold, God, Glory,* Holt, Rinehart and Winston, New York, 1963, 47. C. C. Eldridge criticizes Fieldhouse for inconclusiveness, and although he grants that examining the motives behind imperialism runs the danger of obscuring the subject, so numerous are the causes, he insists an effort at explanation is required that Fieldhouse fails to make. C. C. Eldridge, *British*

The Royal Sussex Regiment. Military heraldry often draws on the heraldry of the honours system – in this case the Garter. The regimental lodge system is familiar to readers of Kipling.

Imperialism in the Nineteenth Century, Hodder & Stoughton, 1978, 146.

6. Gray wrote: "If we are once forced to admit that the tenure of that Empire may not be after all 'Britain's inalienable destiny', but must henceforth depend on the foresight, sagacity, and adaptability of those who are sent out either to bear rule in or to become citizens of . . . then we are forced to ask a still further question: Are we educating these future rulers and future world-citizens in our great schools and "seminaries of useful and religious learning" in the best possible way, so as to secure this foresight . . . ?" Herbert Branston Gray, *The Public Schools and the Empire,* Williams & Norgate, 1913, 23.

7. Philip D. Curtin, "The 'Civilizing Mission'", Philip D. Curtin, ed., *Imperialism,* Macmillan, 1971, 177.

8. E. W. Hornung, "The Field of Philippi", in *A Thief in the Night,* 1905, reptd. 1985 in E. W. Hornung, *The Collected Raffles,* J. M. Dent & Sons, 1985, 345. "Of course Raffles is a public school man, but apart from persuading his ex-fag into a life of crime his outstanding contribution as an Old Boy is to go back to a Founder's Day celebration . . . Once back . . . he robs a bank belonging to an unsporting Old Boy who has ungraciously voted against taking money for a statue of the Founder, presenting his takings under plain cover to the school fund and shaming the miscreant banker into making a separate contribution himself." Jeremy Lewis, "Introduction", *Ibid.,* xii.

9. Evidence for expansion is offered by Lawrence and Jeanne Stone in *An Open Elite? England 1540-1880,* noting that the "landed elite's" attendance at university was at a peak in the mid-seventeenth century and then fell back, and that attendance at the Inns of Court declined to an insignificant role by the nineteenth century, but that the public schools took up the slack. The public schools had the students who a century earlier would

47

Scotch College, Adelaide. Scotch Colleges in several Australian cities achieved prominent public school status.

have been in university. Nineteenth century teachers had the same background that college tutors had in the previous era. Lawrence Stone and Jeanne C. Fawtier Stone, *An Open Elite? England 1540-1880*, Abridged Edition, Oxford University Press, 1986, 170-71.

10. Nadel and Curtis remark: "Whereas 'imperialism' enjoyed at least a genuine if fleeting respectability, 'colonialism' has been weighed down with original sin almost since its inception." *Imperialism and Colonialism*, 3.

11. Herbert Luthy, "Colonization and the Making of Mankind", Nadel and Curtis, eds., *Imperialism and Colonialism*, 35-36.

12. Anthony Wood, *Nineteenth Century Britain*, Second Edition, Longman, Harlow, 1982, 183. Malcolm Falkus and John Gillingham present a helpful map of this growth: "Note in particular, the large number of public schools established after 1860." Caption, Map, "Growth of Education Centres in Great Britain", Malcolm Falkus & John Gillingham, *Historical Atlas of Britain*, Granada, 1981, 207.

13. Wing Commander J. I. Cooper, Officer Commanding Bedford School CCF, Letter, *The Ousel*, Magazine of Bedford School, Vol. LXXXIX, No. 919, March 1985, 21. D. K. Fieldhouse chronicles the vicissitudes of imperialism and the impact of J. A. Hobson's *Imperialism: a Study*, the book which after its appearance in 1902 did so much to shape perceptions of the term. D. K. Fieldhouse, "The New Imperialism: The Hobson-Lenin Thesis Revised", Nadel and Curtis, eds. *Imperialism and Colonialism*, 74-97.

14. Brian Holmes, *Comparative Education: Some Considerations of Method*, George Allen & Unwin, 1981, 137.

15. *Ibid.*, 140.

48

Scotch College, Perth. A black swan imparts
Western Australian flavour.

16. *Ibid.*

17. John Sharp, Headmaster, Prince Rupert School, Wilhelmshaven, *Educating One Nation*, Max Parrish, 1959, 43.

18. Morris, *Pax Britannica*, 23.

19. See Joseph A. Schumpeter, *Imperialism and Social Classes*, Basil Blackwell, Oxford, 1951, esp. 45-56.

20. "Report on Mr. Dundas' Visit to The Persian Gulf", India Office Records R/15/2/210. The India Office Library in London has important archives relating to British educational policy in the Middle East, substantiating public school influence.

21. Morris, *Pax Britannica*, 448.

22. *But the net result of that Primitive Cult,*
    Whatever else may be won,
    Is definite knowledge ere leaving College
    Of the Things that Are Never Done.
Rudyard Kipling, "The Waster", *A Choice of Kipling's Verse*, made by T. S. Eliot, Faber and Faber, 1963, 259.

23. *Illustrated London News*, June 1897.

24. "One (old boy) that springs to mind is Clive of India who was with us for a short while and after whom one of our Houses is named." D. J. Skipper, Headmaster of Merchant Taylors' School, to A. Barakat, Doha Club Library, 21 October 1985.

25. In the early nineteenth century Arabia and public schools were juxtaposed in the writings of Gifford Palgrave, an Old Carthusian, who remarked that Arab and Wahhabi justice were

49

Scotch College, Melbourne. The Southern Cross often indicates an Australian school.

considerably milder than what he had encountered at Charterhouse.

26. Sir Olaf Caroe, who was Foreign Secretary of the Government of India, and Sir Arnold Wilson, the son of a headmaster of Clifton and grandson of a headmaster of King William's.

27. Particularly see Kathryn Tidrick, *Heart-Beguiling Araby*, Cambridge University Press, 1981.

28. S. P. Record, *Proud Century: The first hundred years of Taunton School*, E. Goodman, *Taunton*, 1948, 128. "For 50 years its reputation was local, but during the long headmastership of Dr. Whittaker from 1899 to 1922, it was established as one of the leading Public Schools in the West of England." *Taunton Yearbook*, 1980, 302. Taunton again came into the limelight during the well-publicized headmastership of Dr. John Rae. Mangan notes the use of schoolmaster-pupil analogies in discussion of the Empire, the 'Schoolmaster Syndrome': "As Heussler has remarked of imperial Africa, 'the Briton was an underpaid schoolmaster in an overpopulated school. He lived in the house and took a full part in its life, without ever crossing the line. He knew the boys well and liked them and he sympathized with their problems. His discipline was unyielding and fair, and it was as constant as sun and rain.'" Robert Heussler, *The British in Northern Nigeria*, Oxford University Press, 1968, 182, qtd. Mangan, *The Games Ethic and Imperialism*, 112.

29. G. P. McGregor, *King's College Budo: The First Sixty Years*, Oxford University Press, Nairobi, 1967, 73-74.

30. R. P. Singh, *The Indian Public School*, Sterling Publishers, New Delhi, 1972, 7.

Scotch College, Ontario. Another Scotch College, with the Maple Leaf proclaiming a Canadian location.

31. McGregor, *King's Budo*, 150.

32. Wilfred E. Henn, *A Life So Rich: being a biography of The Rev. Canon P. U. Henn*, Perth, 1982, 16.

33. *Ibid.*, 18.

34. *Ibid.*, 23. See John Cardell-Oliver, "Canon P. U. Henn and Woodardism in Western Australia: Antipodean Modifications of an Anglican Ideal", M.Ed. 1986, The University of Western Australia.

35. Henn, *A Life So Rich*, 73-74.

36. McGregor, *King's Budo*, 4.

37. Charles Allen and Sharada Dwivedi, *Lives of the Indian Princes*, Arrow/Century Hutchinson, 1986, 84.

38. Brian Heeney, *Mission to the Middle Classes: The Woodard Schools, 1848-1891*, SPCK, 28.

39. *Ibid.*, 34-35. Woodard wanted to include Hindustani as part of the curriculum. *Ibid.*, 106.

40. Patrick Maguire, *A Brief Sketch of Development at Cranleigh*, Cranleigh School, nd, 3. An historian of Truro School related: "A noteworthy happening of the Pre-War (WWI) period was the arrival of many pupils from overseas, the Argentine, Uruguay, Brazil, Mandalay, South Africa, Ireland and the Channel Islands. Mention of the Argentine prompts memory of the Tregeas, five of them, essentially footballers; from India came the four Gilpins, particularly good at cricket. Nigel Baker, ed., *Truro School*, Blackfords, Truro, 1980, 12.

41. qtd. Isabel Quigly, *The Heirs of Tom Brown: The English School Story*, Oxford University Press, 1984, 98.

St.Patrick's Schools, Nova Scotia. These well known sister schools are heraldically differentiated by the women using a lozenge frame.

42. "Obviously, the children of expatriates may in most cases have a very strong claim to a boarding school education, since that has been the peculiar English (and sometimes other British) custom since the days of Empire. The other world colonizers of former times, however, and the present world powers with large overseas staffs, do not as a rule send their children back to the homeland for a schooling away from their parents. Instead, they establish high schools, *lycees* and the like in the cities of the countries where they work, to include provision for the locals too." King, *Other Schools*, 231.

43. Philip Woodruff, *The Founders*, Jonathan Cape, 1953, 279. These were significant as early indications of British interest in establishing educational institutions in India.

44. Singh, *The Indian Public School*, 4. In 1969 the Indian Public Schools Conference, formerly the Indian Headmasters' Conference, had 44 members. *Ibid.*, 112-13.

45. Morris wrote: "They were assiduous and highly successful brainwashers. As the Anglo-Oriental College at Aligarh said of its curriculum, its object was not merely the formation of character and the encouragement of manly pursuits, but the fostering among the boys of 'an active sense of their duty as loyal subjects'. Often the anti-intellectual prejudices of the lesser English schools were faithfully reproduced, as was the Spartan discipline . . ." Morris, *Pax Britannica*, 141.

46. Said, *Orientalism*, 244.

47. McGregor, *King's Budo*, 23.

48. *Ibid.*, 23-24.

49. Henry Weatherhead, the first headmaster of King's, wrote: "Too many missionaries expected a kind of seminary to turn out

52

Aligarh. A great force in Muslim education's revival in India, Aligarh eventually became a university – as did a number of other Indian schools.

native clergy or Church workers. But the Bishop was I think as keen as I was on the adaptation of our English Public School method to the Africa race." *Ibid.*, 12.

50. *Ibid.*, 29-30.

51. McGregor wrote: "Royal Coronations are not commonly part of a school's tradition so at least a brief description will not be out of place, the more so as Daudi had been a frequent visitor to Budo, and after his 'educational tour' of Britain in 1912 had intimated that he wished to be regarded as an Old Budonian. A few months before his Investiture he had accepted the office of President of the newly formed Old Budonian Association." *Ibid.*, 35-36. McGregor quotes Elspeth Huxley in 1963: "Budo was founded about half a century ago for chiefs' sons, and since then anyone who's anyone has sent his sons to be shaped into true Uganda gentlemen by its first rate academic discipline—only the best masters intellectually and morally have taught there—and its muscular Christianity in the Dr. Arnold tradition (*Sic*). Now Uganda's establishment is almost solidly Old Budonian." *Ibid.*, 158.

52. William Redman Duggan, *Our Neighbors Upstairs: The Canadians*, Nelson-Hall, Chicago, 1979, 287.

53. McGregor, *King's Budo*, 40.

54. *Trinity College School News*, Vol. 1, No. 1, 1985, 14.

55. Philip W.Jackson, "Secondary School for the Privileged Few", *Daedalus*, Vol. 110, No. 4, 123-24.

56. A sociologist of education at the University of the West Indies remarked: "Furthermore, since a number of illustrious Jamaicans (including three of the five prime ministers) attended these schools, there is vicarious prestige to be gained by those

Jamaica. In 1983 Prime Minister Edward Seaga unsuccessfully tried to jettison the national arms from which much Jamaican school heraldry derives. "Can the crushed and extinct Arawaks represent the dauntless character of Jamaicans?" he asked. "Does the low-slung, near extinct crocodile, a cold-blooded reptile, symbolize the warm soaring spirt of Jamaicans?" Critics suggested "entwined marijuana plants against a background of US dollar bills".

who attend the same schools." Aggrey Brown, *Color, Class, and Politics in Jamaica*, Transaction Books, New Brunswick, New Jersey, 1979, 86-87.

57. McGregor, *King's Budo*, 12.

The International Order of Job's Daughters is sponsored by the Freemasons of some countries to provide girls with a lodge affiliation.

CHAPTER THREE

TALISMANS AND TOTEMS

The tall hat is no longer worn except on Sundays,
but the praepostors continue to carry sticks as a
mark of distinction.
                              Annals of Shrewsbury School.

One of those public-school ties which carry
important messages between all true Englishmen
                              D. Jordan, *Black Account.*

Talismans and totems were central to school life, although often they appeared ludicrous to the uninitiated.[1] Far from being incidental, they acquired a lifelong significance. Just what they were, and how they became the inspiration of later Imperial wizardry, is central to any consideration of the public school's influence on the Empire.

While distinctions can be drawn between the export throughout the Empire of trappings such as blazers, badges, and prizes, and the export of *ideology*, there is not such a difference as might be supposed. The apparently inconsequential trappings were crucial to sustaining Imperial control.[2]

Admittedly the overseas school ritualism sometimes degenerated into a concern for haberdashery, but those who cherished uniforms and colours patterned after the English schools came close to the truth of the public school experience. The talismans, while seemingly minor, were a

Reed's School, Cobham, Surrey. Design by Old Etonian Reynolds Stone, 1809-1979, distinguished heraldic artist and son and grandson of Eton schoolmasters.

shorthand for values that the schools sought to instil. They were embraced even by humble state-maintained schools in the hopes that the power and prestige would rub off.

Their use emphasizes how the past lives into the present through objects. Its artifacts are the substratum which underlie ideology. In the case of the public schools, the ritualism that was so carefully handed down guaranteed that the essence of the schools themselves was being continued. Masters and boys by adopting it reaffirmed the past. The place of ritual has been unappreciated or comically cartooned, but it did much to ensure the perpetuation of the schools and the Empire.

Dressing for Dinner

The much repeated story about the British wearing formal dress for dinner in completely incongruous surroundings is an instance of how the trivial became talismanic. The British Political Agent in Kuwait from 1920 to 1929, Major James Carmichael More, did in fact dress nightly for dinner. Dame Violet Dickson recorded how he changed into formal evening clothes even when dining alone with his wife.[3]

While this particular kind of behaviour has always been a favourite subject for a *Punch* cartoon, evening dress had an Imperial function:

> . . . it was necessary to 'keep up standards'. This of course did influence us and it is easy to make fun of it. But there was a good reason. Aldous Huxley, on a tourist's visit, noticed that many of the inhabitants of India might have sat as models for the old man of Thermopylae who never did anything properly. And in a sense it was by doing things properly—more often at least than most Indians—that the British had established themselves and that so few ruled so many with so slight a use of overt force.[4]

56

Masonic candidate. Initiates were clothed in simple white costume surrendering metal objects and monies to emphasise dependence on the lodge. Members, in contrast, wore evening dress.

The Imperial reliance on an identifying uniform recalled school life, where the number of unbuttoned buttons was fraught with meaning. The costumes of masters and boys were part of a drama. At Australia's Camberwell school:

> The maintenance of an aura of differentness, apartness, of infallibility gave the leader his magic dignity. Manners were ritualised (the Englishman dressing for dinner in a remote clearing in the Borneo jungle), for the ritual was the way to beauty and beauty the way to harmony . . .[5]

This magic was widely sought by public schools abroad, as at Camberwell and at King's Budo, where the Old Budonians' Association in 1914 warned members about the old boy jacket: "It is not to be worn when going to work or to try and impress other people, because this will only cause ill-feeling among non-Budonians, and we shall be despised by the Europeans and the older Baganda."[6]

The O.B.s were right that copying of uniforms and other superficials sometimes earned contempt rather than approval. It seemed that the more slavishly the refinements were copied, the greater was the ridicule.[7] The hostility was not reserved for foreigners, who were not so much despised as regarded with the sense of superiority that the English had for Scots. The public school man was democratic in his scorn, and had the same contempt for minor schools in England that tried to 'put on airs' as he did for struggling colonial schools.[8]

Some of Britain's colonial subjects persisted despite the rebuffs in displaying an almost childish desire to please, a longing for recognition. The flattery was dismissed with irritation by those it flattered. The native obsession with Imperial ritualism is examined in *A Passage to India*, in particular where E. M. Forster records a dialogue between the British headmaster Fielding and Professor Godbole, an Indian. Forster deftly makes the point that everyone's preoccupation with such window dressing is part of the waste of colonialism.

57

Symbol of the Lodge of Perfection, which in the Ancient and Accepted Rite of Freemasonry works the degrees of fourth through fourteenth.

Godbole comes to Fielding for advice about starting a school, but finds him preoccupied with the serious criminal charges that have landed his friend Aziz in jail. Nonetheless, Godbole persists:

> "The point—the point on which I desire your help is this: what name should be given to the school?"
>
> "Really,—I have no names for schools in my head. I can think of nothing but our poor Aziz. Have you grasped that at the present moment he is in prison?"
>
> "Oh yes, Oh no, I do not expect an answer to my question now. I only meant that when you are at leisure you might think the matter over, and suggest two or three alternative titles for schools. I had thought of the 'Mr.Fielding High School', but failing that, the 'King-Emperor George the Fifth'."[9]

The public school traditions were imitated in the hopes they brought with them the cachet and social advantages of the schools. The minutiae of school ritualism are the spoor of the schools' influence. An examination of a few of the many public school customs and how they influenced the Empire is appropriate.

Scholarships

One observation that can be made about public school traditions is that things are seldom as simple as they seem. A case in point is the schools' seemingly innocuous scholarship system. It was administered as a sort of ritual and became a ceremonial portal.

Scholarships were a well known part of public school life, but they are much misunderstood. Like many other school customs, they cannot be accepted on face value. They were not simply a way of letting the children of poor parents attend prestige institutions. The stylized competition for them, the

Geelong Church of England Grammar School, Australia. Prince Charles attended for a year, although most of his schooling was at Scotland's Gordonstoun.

liturgies accompanying their actual award, and the attire that identified the recipients argue that they were part of the schools' pageantry.

They seldom constituted a way that worthy boys from the lower classes could climb to distinction. During mid-nineteenth century educational reforms, the Clarendon Commissioners were well aware that many endowments technically for the aid of the poor had been usurped.[10] The Commission and the schools refused to enforce the wishes of donors, and the trusts were used by the middle classes.

In retrospect, whether the majority of the scholarships awarded went to the disadvantaged seems very doubtful. Instead of providing financial aid to those who needed it, the system when scrutinized often revealed itself as a closed circle involving preparatory schools, old boys, and the Empire. The scholarships were not, as a practical matter, open to the lower classes. With the rise of the preparatory school from the 1860s onwards, boys educated elsewhere had no chance of winning a scholarship.

A purpose that the scholarships did advance substantially was the rejuvenation of the Imperial services. Numerous stipends assisted colonial personnel in sending their sons back to England for public schooling, boys who in many cases then pursued Imperial careers. The Old Pauline of India Scholarship was: ". . . from time to time available for the benefit of the sons of an Old Pauline entering the Senior School, preference being given to an Old Pauline who has resided in India or Pakistan."[11] Wellington College provided scholarships for the sons of deceased officers "in the army of the Hon. East India Company".[12] The Knightly Scholarships at Tonbridge were for sons of ICS officers. Elizabeth College in Guernsey had a scholarship founded in 1869 "particularly to help boys entering the Indian Civil Service".[13]

Such scholarships may have had the additional effect of discouraging any interest in aiding education overseas. Local education might have been more supported if the British had relied less on the public schools at home and educated their sons where they were working. The government financial

59

St.Paul's. Although mainly a day school, St.Paul's has consistently been in the top echelon.

assistance enabling the Imperial civil services to send their children to English public schools contributed to this neglect.

The scholarships created for the children of civil servants and old boys ensured a continuing supply of those whose families had associations with both the public schools and with serving the Empire, but whose loyalty would be to schools in England. Such awards were created at the same time as the schools' expansion and the Empire's acquisitions. Besides grants for those whose fathers were in the civil services, scholarships were founded for anyone with a father in the armed forces, eligibility for which of course included the children of many civil officials who held military commissions.[14] For example, the Lugard Scholarships at Rossall were for "sons of serving or retired members of the Colonial Colleges and children of serving and retired members of the Armed Forces".[15]

Scholarships, it thus can be concluded, were often elitist. In their late Victorian form they were not a hoary tradition but a social innovation, and they should not be confused with the simple earlier awards of financial aid. The entrance examinations to public schools presented an overwhelming obstacle unless a child had attended a preparatory school. In impoverished India and Africa, their introduction had the same effects as in England. They automatically excluded the poor because without a middle class background, preparatory school, or expensive tutoring, a child could not hope for examination success.[16]

Prizes

As well as scholarships, prizes proliferated and became a well established part of school life. They had an Imperial counterpart in the proliferation of orders and medals that took place. A CSI or CMG was the counterpart of a prize day award at the old school.

The subject of school competitions for the prizes was often Imperial ("One School and One Empire") and the prizes were

Rossall. The school produced a number of bishops; church ties are indicated by the mitre.

frequently books on similar themes. Athleticism may have been a theme of public school history, but sportsmanship could be strained when awards were contested. A prize dispute at Eton was actually given as a reason for Curzon's resignation as Viceroy, the ancient origin of his quarrels with the Secretary of State for India, Sir John Broderick. When the Governor of Cyprus, Sir Ronald Storrs, had his house burned by a crowd that blamed him for pro-Turkish sentiments, the most lamented of his treasures was his Homer won as a prize at Charterhouse.[17]

Most public schools had endowed prizes. Prize-day was a ubiquitous custom, accompanied by much pomp and palaver. At Budo:

> The first Speech Day was held on Easter Monday 1908, and with the Kabaka and the Governor, Sir Hesketh Bell, present, the third year boys must have felt that being an Old Budonian was really going to matter . . . The Governor told the boys that he would be watching their progress carefully after they left Budo, and would be ready to help them.[18]

The whole idea of such observances was to duplicate as much as possible the "home" counterparts. After one such Budo ceremony, the headmaster smugly noted: "I doubt if we ever get so close to the atmosphere of an English public school as upon these occasions . . ."[19]

Bearing in mind the considerable popularity of such awards in the schools, it is not surprising to discover that in a remote region like the Arabian Gulf there were similar prize schemes, despite the arid surroundings and the more pressing need for textbooks and writing paper.[20] Just how momentous these matters were viewed is illustrated by the concern accorded school prizes in the Gulf in April 1947.

India, to which the Gulf was tied, was in turmoil because of the British withdrawal. The political fortunes of the Middle East were consequently in grave doubt. Notwithstanding, the

61

Eton. Eton's lilies are one of the most famous of school emblems.

British Agent at Kuwait at the time was in worried correspondence with the Political Resident over prizes for the schools. Should they be silver cups? If cups were given, would they be upstaged by whatever others might donate? Would giving cups establish a *precedent*?[21] The Resident decided that he preferred giving cash, and a series of presentations was duly arranged.[22] Reward was integral to Imperial ritualism.

The Tour

Ideas travelled about the Empire but so did people. The spread of public school influence received a considerable boost from a variety of schoolboy awards for travel. The most famous excursions were those promoted by Winchester's headmaster, M. J. Rendall, but there were numerous others.

Rendall embarked on these trips with the energy of a landlord inspecting his property. (His personal travels took him to such remote reaches as the Sinai desert and Nile Valley, but even there he found Old Wykehamists who entertained him.) As Chairman of *Public School Tours to the Empire*, he organized twenty large-scale expeditions. They were scrupulously planned and each took about four months. Some circumnavigated the globe. Old boy connections smoothed the way, and provided introductions to Governors and Prime Ministers.

The boys were inspecting what they could be running in a few years' time, but there was little attempt to introduce them to the local customs.[23] They were there to learn the Imperial ones. Entertained by Government House and the local British clubs, they visited overseas schools and paired off for picnics with old boys of their own English schools, they returned home flush with exotic but misleading impressions.

Rendall's tours were not the only ones that enabled schoolboys to view the Empire,[24] but they were among the most publicized. Another, less publicized category was the jaunts financed by scholarships which enabled boys to plan

62

Magdalen College School, Oxford. While hardly a rival of Eton, Magdalen also displays lilies.

their own itinerary. Typically, the Dewar Travelling Scholarship at Rugby sought "applications if their plans are well-advanced and if their contribution to School life has been sound". The Travelling Bursary at Taunton went to "the boy who proposed the itinerary and object which the Head Master considered most desirable".[25]

If boys sometimes had opportunities to see the Empire, headmasters who were so inclined most certainly did.[26] Any list of them would surely include Harrow's J. E. C. Welldon,[27] a zealot who saw nothing strange about leading non-Harrovian congregations in prayers for the school. He was one of the best travelled of all headmasters,[28] and his Imperial enthusiasm led him into a tumultuous career as head of the Anglican Church in India.[29] There his proselytizing for English education was one of the aspects of a still poorly understood quarrel with his lifelong friend and the then Viceroy, Lord Curzon.[30]

Rendall and Welldon are famous traveling heads who were at home in the corners of the Empire, but there were many other masters and boys whose trips spread the public school message. This exchange achieved new dimensions after World War I when the English-Speaking Union organized schoolmaster and schoolboy yearly exchanges on a large scale. Still another development was the Kinsmen Trust, which after World War II brought Canadians and Americans (of which the author was one) to leading English schools. The whole subject awaits its Boswell.

The King of Arms

Since headmasters, masters, and boys travelled throughout the Empire, it is not surprising that fulsome commemorations of the public school heritage can be found overseas in stained glass, mortuary art, textbooks, bookplates, and armorial bearings. Outstanding amongst these totems, the coats-of-arms were, depending on one's outlook, a byzantine or engaging field.

63

The Kings of Arms. From left: Garter, Lyon, and Clarenceux.

No public school in England or elsewhere for that matter was complete without its display of heraldry. *The Heraldry Gazette*, "The Official Newsletter of The Heraldry Society", provides numerous examples of what can only be called public school heraldic hysteria.[31] The *Gazette*, which had a penchant about schools' unauthorized use of arms, has by no means reconciled itself to the waning of Imperial authority. It fights a stout rearguard action to keep the former colonies in heraldic line: "St. George's School, Vancouver, has become the second private school in the Province to receive a *lawful* grant of Arms."[32]

This armorialism cost substantial sums, first for the detailed research into appropriate devices to represent the applicant, and then for artists to render them, and finally for official proclamation of the design by the Heralds. The head of a state school, beset by budget problems for necessities, would not put a grant of arms on his priority list.

What is more remarkable is that a school thousands of miles from London would seek a grant from a King of Arms and confirmation by the College of Heralds. This dramatizes the ritualistic concern of the public schools.

The display of arms did not cease when a country wor independence. St. George's is not the only overseas school to petition for its gules and dragons.[33] While the flourishing of armorial bearings by schools goes back centuries, the new nineteenth-century schools made the adoption of arms a first item of business.[34] As with some of their English counterparts, overseas school historians went into excruciating detail about their institutions' arms, which they seemed to feel provided an assurance of legitimacy.

An instance of this is a complicated discussion of the difficulties in designing the school's armorial achievement in *Schoolroom and Playing Field*, the centennial history of Timaru School in New Zealand. It ends with the relieved announcement that "the King of Arms in London granted . . . a new coat which, although based on the previous design, conformed fully to the best heraldic practice."[35] Similarly, the historian of Brighton Grammar School in Victoria, Australia,

64

Timaru, New Zealand. Another notable overseas school taking the proper course and obtaining a grant from the College in London.

proudly discusses its ornate Arms, reproduced in colour along with the full archaic grant, beginning, ". . . Know ye therefore that We the said Garter, Clarenceux and Norroy and Ulster in pursuance of His Grace's Warrant . . .".[36] The histories of heraldry in the brochures that schools sent to parents sometimes occupy more pages than discussions of the science laboratories or curriculum.

Schools with Scottish connections, no matter how distant from Edinburgh, could and did apply to the Lord Lyon rather than to the Heralds in London. When Knox Grammar School near Sydney made the attempt, after years of innocently using a homegrown design, it got a nasty response: ". . . we do not register other people's invention . . . really the whole basis of a Knox Grammar School armorial bearings or badge should be reconsidered and brought into conformity with heraldic principles."[37]

This concern about *Escallops in base Or* and *Crosses crosslet fitchy* recalls Professor Godbole's anxieties over what to call his school—an obsession for the right rituals. The same obsession cropped up in the Arabian Gulf, and as a relic of it the Emirate of Bahrain's schools still display a positively Arthurian coat, the legacy of the Adviser in the 1920s, Sir Charles Belgrave.[38]

There is nothing sinister about all this (if an heraldic pun is permissible), but behind the petitions to the Kings of Arms was the idea that acquiring such totems produced a public school. This was not altogether wrong. Rather than treating school ritual as incidental, its power must be acknowledged. Woe to anyone who tried to change the totems under the mistaken impression that they had no substance.

In the Middle Ages, heraldry performed practical functions, giving a quick idea of the social position of the bearer. The public schools' rituals in many ways performed the same function. J. A. Mangan pointed out how they became: ". . . established symbols of differentiation which allegedly created a sense of tradition and hierarchy."[39]

Bahrain. Sir Charles Belgrave's design is still used – interesting since Bahrain in 1971, like the other Gulf shaikhdoms, became independent.

Mortuary Arts and the Public Schools

Highly symbolic was the custom, already referred to in the case of Henn, of burying of masters and old boys in the cloisters or chapel of their school—or in the extreme case of having a mausoleum as a focal point of the school.[40] This was peculiar to the public schools and copied overseas. As a custom it deserves emphasis, because it says so much about the nature of public schools.

As mentioned, Arnold is buried in Rugby Chapel, Sanderson in Oundle's, and, taking a colonial example, Henn in Guildford Chapel. Percival rests in Clifton Chapel and visitors to Eton Chapel see monuments to a profusion of old boys and masters resting within and without. The suggestion of interring anyone in the confines of an ordinary local authority school would be regarded as macabre.

For old boys of reflective disposition, this interest in the funereal extended to making mortuary art into a hobby that perhaps pleasantly recalled schooldays. Monuments to departed old boys who died abroad could be visited, wreaths laid, and if need be, the tombs restored.[41] The *Radleian* informed O.R.s that Imperial monuments were being repaired in India, Pakistan, Bangladesh, Burma, Sri Lanka, and Malaysia, and that they had an invitation to join the effort of their fellow O.R.s.[42]

The Old School Tie

The talismans and totems—the prize books and uniforms, the crests and badges and indeed the old boy cufflinks—were the props of a unique stagecraft. Of all of them, the foremost was dress. In fact, the most famous totem was and is the old school tie.

However, the old boys did not limit their regalia to ties. Old Tauntonian Society officers had chains, badges, and collars,[43] and the ceremonial appearances of their presidents can be compared with Curzon's Viceregal landing at Sharjah for his

Knight Bachelor's Badge. Only sanctioned in 1926, this is worn either as a breast badge or pendent from a neck ribbon.

durbar with the Gulf Sheikhs in 1903: ". . . his full dress and gold collar of the Star of India contrasted oddly with his efforts to board the wobbling launch."[44] The Imperial penchant for fancy dress owed something to the public school zealousness for dressing up.[45]

Conversely, the current appearance of boys in mufti at schools of the stature of Rugby raises the point whether there has emerged an inverse snobbery whereby a true public school talisman will be the lack of a uniform, while the local authority schools cling to blazers. The new exceptions to informality are intriguing—at Christ's Hospital the boys themselves have steadfastly insisted on their medieval garb.

Selection of colours involved grave deliberation. After debate in 1906 by the Old Tauntonians (who seem to have been particularly concerned over sartorial affairs): "A design, consisting of a combination of the School Colours (royal blue and navy), and a thin line of gold was decided upon for hatbands, sashes, and ties. Twenty-one years later, after continuing lengthy and heated discussions at Annual General Meetings, an official blazer similar in colours to the existing tie was authorized . . ."[46]

For anyone interested in exploring the ties of school history, James Laver's monumental history deals with the antecedents and vagaries of several hundred: "Warwick School . . . Crested tie for members of association only. Two striped ties for Old Boys generally. Emblem—white bear and ragged staff, and gold portcullis."[47] The dominions and colonies are ecumenically treated and thanks to elaborate cross-referencing one discerns that thin multiple stripes of silver, red and yellow on navy identify an old boy of Melbourne Grammar School, avoiding confusion with the thin multiple stripes of silver, red and silver on navy of St. Andrew's College in Ontario. (One of whose old boys was the first native Canadian Governor-General of Canada, Vincent Massey.)[48]

Mr. Laver put the blame for the bright striped world of symbolic ties on the public schools. Among the first he asserted was Wellington College's, the colours taken from the

St.George's Lodge, Paris. Established just two months before the beginning of World War 1, this English-speaking lodge has prospered and meets in a handsome building in Neuilly.

ribbon of the Crimean War medal.[49] He noted that the development of the blazer coincided with the old school tie and that the entire movement was part of a grand hierarchical principle that "clothes and the decoration of clothes ought to *mean something*".[50] There were limits. The appearance of made-up bow ties in the Patent Office Records for 1864 produced a rare excess of emotion from this sartorial historian: "The cads!"[51]

Clothing had the additional purpose of marking distinctions within schools that were as vital as the distinctions between schools. The tie situation at Sherborne seemed typical where there was a school prefects' tie, a tie for each major sport, ties for prefects from each of the half dozen boarding houses, and a tie for the old boys' sporting association.[52] This concern produced an ultra sensitivity to the variations. With such attention to symbolism, it is not surprising that the effects were lifelong.

Into Adult Life

The old boys carried their rituals into adult life. One notes a public school inspection and review (see *Review of Tonbridge School Officers' Training Corps Band*, page 69) and then a review of colonial troops (see *His Excellency Sir Hubert and Lady Young Review the Honour Guard*, page 70). The similarities are striking.

The old school ties were the sartorial indication of having passed the course in rule by ritual. They also indicated the binding ties of lifelong friendships and were the more notable for their unobtrusiveness. That men should go through their lives wearing a symbol of their adolescence is extremely significant. It is not happenstance that a modern classic, Anthony Powell's serial novel *A Dance to the Music of Time*, starts with describing the characters in their school and then follows them, as their school friendships ripple through their

Euphrates Lodge. Founded in 1795, it enjoys a close relationship with Tigris Lodge. A number of members fought under the Duke of Wellington in the Peninsular War.

Tonbridge School Officers' Training Corps Band, 1938. When this author was at Tonbridge, the corps seemed more prepared for celebrations than for combat. They paraded when old boy military leaders such as Lord Ironside, or the Governors – the Master and Court of the Skinners' Company – made visits. (Skinners' Arms, left).

His Excellency Sir Hubert and Lady Young Review the Honour Guard, Trinidad, 1938. An Old Etonian, Sir Hubert was involved in T.E. Lawrence's Hejaz operations and then served in the Colonial Office's Middle East Department before becoming Counsellor to the High Commissioner in Iraq, 1929-32; Governor of Nyasaland, 1934-38; and Governor of Trinidad and Tobago, 1938-42. Imperial authority relied on such pageantry.

careers like a stone's ripples in a pond. Powell's characters never escape their schooldays. Neither did the rulers of the Empire.

Putting Everything Together

The incongruous rituals carried to far ends of the world are an easy butt of humour, but in the Empire the emphasis on ritualism was critical to controlling the native populations. Dressing for dinner was doubly impressive when the temperature hovers at 50° Centigrade. [53]

For full effectiveness the different symbols had to be integrated. At school the numerous special events offered unique opportunities to do this. The frequency with which royalty and nobility graced public school occasions showed the significance attached to the schools and gave the boys a tutoring in how to stage Imperial gaudies.

One such affair was reported in the *Times Educational Supplement* for 6 August, 1938. It was a summer camp being held for public school boys and selected ordinary youths at Southwold, the purpose being to integrate the public and non-public school boys much as camps are run today to bring together Protestant and Catholic children from Belfast. A royal visit was programmed and King George VI landed from the Royal Yacht, "with a destroyer in unobtrusive attendance". His (unobtrusive) destroyer hovering in the background, the King processed ashore, where:

> Waiting there to greet him were the Home Secretary, Sir Samuel Hoare, in white flannels; the Lord Lieutenant of the County, Lord Stradbroke; Mr. Robert Hyde, director of the Industrial Welfare Society; the Camp Chief, Captain J. G. Peterson; and the Camp Bursar, Mr. Pitman.

71

Broxbourne Grammar School uses the head of a badger or "brock" with wavy bars representing a "bourne" and antlers of a hart for Hertfordshire.

Such pomp and ritual were integral to the running of the Empire. Special functions such as the King's visit provided the opportunity to blend the ingredients. Public school speech days, cornerstone-layings, visits of notables, chapel ceremonies and other pageantry instructed the future directors of Imperial ceremonies. There was no other place where tutoring was offered in such detail about the *de rigueur* protocol and etiquette that embryo governors needed.

The interest in such subjects was one that carried over into adult life. The *Ampleforth Journal* reminded O.A.s:

> Ampleforth is always well represented in English Royal and State ceremonial with the present Duke of Norfolk as Earl Marshal of England, Sir John Johnston as Comptroller of the Lord Chamberlain's Office, Major General Lord Michael Fitzalan Howard as Gold Stick to the Queen, Henry Paston Bedingfield as Rouge Croix Pursuivant at the College of Arms . . . However, Ampleforth is equally well represented in Scottish ceremonial as it was in July at the Thistle Service in St. Giles Cathedral. Sir John Johnston masterminded the arrangements; the Marquess of Lothian was in command of the attachment of the Queen's Body Guard for Scotland (The Royal Company of Archers), of which Sir Hew Hamilton-Dalrymple is the Adjutant, shortly to retire after twenty years of distinguished service; Peter Beauclerk Dewar served as Falkland Pursuivant Extraordinary and John George assisted with the seating arrangements.[54]

As will be seen, public school freemasonry offered a special training in integrating the rituals of Imperial administration. So did games, the role of which J. A. Mangan has thoroughly examined.[55] Freemasons and athletes might not recognize their common ground, but the two systems have resemblances, including a certain clannishness and self-

Ampleforth. One of those premier Roman Catholic public schools which are far removed socially from the run-of-the-mill parochial schools.

satisfied superiority. They were strong components of the new ritualism.

A Substitute for Gunboats

The ritual emphasis on superiority was vital because the ability to enforce politics by force was limited. The British used ceremonies as a substitute for gunboats. A colourful example was Lord Curzon's spectacular and celebrated visit to the Arabian Gulf in 1903 when he appeared frequently in magnificent costumes. It was one of many but all the more noteworthy for the sterility of the desert background. It conveyed, as many Imperial ceremonies did, exactly the impression of magnificence intended.

Public school life was a rehearsal for this Imperial show. It is not surprising that the Empire's rulers such as Curzon thought that abracadabra came with the job, because it was part of their schooldays. The ritualism was integral to their remarkable self-confidence. Any doubts about just how integral are quelled by the extraordinary extent of public school freemasonry.

Arms of the College of Preceptors, chartered in 1849 and along with other functions providing nominals and gowns as well as qualifications for those who did not attend university.

NOTES—CHAPTER THREE

1. Edmund King puts it: "They are not expected actually to *train* anyone for anything; yet they may well equip people in the social (and even economic) struggle for important positions if they confer on ambitious young men and women the *talismans*' which are locally most prized—knowledge of the Classics, deft references to literature and the arts, a superior air and an upper-class drawl, or whatever it is that marks the top person. At the risk of over-simplification, we recognize these characteristics in the English 'Public' Schools . . ." King, *Other Schools and Ours*, 39.

2. The Tonbridge School Shop offers O.T. crested cufflinks, tankards, tie clips, key rings, and blazer buttons (large or small size). Mrs. R. A. Newble, Manager, to P. J. Rich, 18 February 1986.

3. Violet Dickson, *Forty Years in Kuwait*, George Allen & Unwin, 1971, 75.

4. Charles Allen, ed., *Plain Tales from the Raj: Images of British India in the Twentieth Century*, Futura, 1985, 17.

5. Hansen, *By Their Deeds*, 41.

6. McGregor, *King's Budo*, 37.

7. Richard Symonds, *The British and Their Successors: A*

Portcullis Lodge, Langport. The lodge takes its name from the blazon of Lady Margaret Beaufort, mother of Henry VII. It served in the seventeenth century as a grammar school.

Study in the Development of the Government Services in the New States, Faber and Faber, 1966, 39.

8. Morris remarked in *Pax Britannica*: "The emergence of Western-educated Indians, speaking a flowery English of their own, casually failing to recognize their own pre-ordained place in the order of things—the arrival on the scene of these bouncy protégés did nothing to draw the British closer to their wards, but only exacerbated their aloofness." Morris, 140.

9. E. M. Forster, *A Passage to India*, Abinger Edition, 1979, 184-85.

10. "But they did not see how the poor were to be made part of a public school. If they were to become oppidans (paying students, usually associated with Eton but used elsewhere), expenses would have to be lowered and teaching efficiency thus harmed . . . short of destroying entirely the upper-class character of schools, which, of course, they had no intention of doing, the best way to cut the Gordian knot was to abolish entirely the traditional rights of the poor. They did this by recommending that entrance to the foundations of all schools be made a matter of competitive examination, a solution both entirely in accordance with the *laissez-faire* business ideals of the Victorian upper classes and singularly effective for securing its end, since a good deal of expensive preparation was necessary to pass public school entrance examinations." Edward C. Mack, *Public Schools and British Opinion Since 1860*, Columbia University Press, 1941 (reprinted Greenwood Press, Westport, 1971), 31-32.

11. J. F. Burnet, ed., *Public & Preparatory Schools Yearbook 1980*, Adam & Charles Black, 1980, 280.

12. *Ibid.*, 323.

13. V. G. Collenette, *Elizabeth College*, Guernsey Press, 1963, 25.

Common Seal, Corporation of Etwall Hospital and Repton School. Like other schools, as this example indicates, Repton started as part of a charitable foundation that included a hospital or almshouse, lending irony to the school's subsequent exclusion of the poor – a development to which Mack alludes in the above quote.

14. Many of the Indian Political Service men had Army commissions, as did Indian Civil Service officers.

15. Burnet, ed., *Public Schools Yearbook*, 252.

16. I am grateful to Mr. Terry Sutcliffe for emphasizing the point about just how intimidating disadvantaged candidates for scholarship examinations find the usual examination surroundings, so different from anything they have previously encountered.

17. ". . . as for the things that went in Cyprus, perhaps they were taken because I cared for them too much . . ." James Morris, *Farewell the Trumpets: An Imperial Retreat*, Penguin Books, Harmondsworth, 1984, 394.

18. McGregor, *King's Budo*, 27.

19. *Ibid.*, 28.

20. IOR: R/5/5/198, "Kuwait Education", 161, 176.

21. *Ibid.*, M. O. Tandy to W. R. Hay, 8 April 1947.

22. *Ibid.*, W. R. Hay to M. O. Tandy, 21 April 1947. Then Tandy wrote to the Amir of Kuwait to settle the judges for the competition and other particulars. *Ibid.*, See M. O. Tandy to His Highness Sheikh Sir Ahmed Al Jabir, KCSI, KCIE, Ruler of Kuwait, 19 May 1947. *Ibid.*

23. Mangan wrote about Rendall: "Quite simply his concept of community was caste-ridden. A major obligation lay on the shoulders of the occidental 'Brahmin', the Anglo-Saxon, to exert a 'benevolent and firm control . . . upon the new, weaker and backward nations'. In Britain the public schoolboy was in precisely the same relationship to the elementary school pupil. He had the same obligations." Mangan, *The Games Ethic*, 30.

Baldwyn Lowick Lodge. An English lodge in Malaysia: a book on Masonic heraldry in various countries is much needed. See page 36.

24. Record, *Proud Century*, 161.

25. "Dewar Scholarships", *The Rugby Meteor*, Rugby School, 1985, 24. Also Record, *Proud Century*, 238.

26. Mangan wrote that Welldon was the "most eloquent, persistent and opinioned spokesman on the schools and imperialism". Mangan, *The Games Ethic*, 33. Welldon on one occasion pontificated: "An English headmaster, as he looks to the future of his pupils, will not forget that they are to be the citizens of the greatest empire under heaven." He left Harrow to be Bishop of Calcutta, owing his appointment to Lord George Hamilton, Secretary of State for India and both a Harrow governor and old boy. Kenneth Rose, *Curzon: A Most Superior Person*, Macmillan, 1985, 334.

27. Welldon and Curzon attributed their interest in India to Eton. Curzon told an Old Etonian dinner that he dated his enthusiasm for going there to a lecture at the College by Sir James Stephen. *Ibid.*, 335.

28. See *Ibid.*, 194.

29. Welldon had a keen sense of ritual. Mary Curzon describes his enthronement in Calcutta: "The service was magnificent and began with the Archdeacon taking the Bishop by the hand and conducting him to the throne, which is hung in purple. As Welldon's robes were flaming red over a white surplice it was very brilliant." Mary Curzon to family, 2 February 1899, qtd. John Bradley, ed., *Lady Curzon's India: Letters of a Vicereine*, Weidenfeld and Nicolson, 1985, 28.

30. Lord Curzon wrote to his wife: "Meanwhile Secretary of State has sent to me a proposal with consent of King, Prime Min. & Archbishop of Canterbury to make Welldon an archbishop & has asked my opinion. It puts me in a very difficult position. I can scarcely tell you the hubbub that has been caused in the Indian press by Welldon's speeches in England.

Bosnia. No political upheaval occurs without symbolic upheaval. The new nation of Bosnia-Herzegovina has adopted the arms of Stephen Dabisha, King of Bosnia in 1397. The flag is this shield on a white background.

He is denounced by every newspaper, English & Indian. They think he is coming back with a policy of State proselytising and the English Bills in Education. I am supposed to have sent him home in order to secure assent to this new policy, and if he comes back an Archbishop everyone will imagine that he has succeeded. He is doing me & the Govt. an immense amount of harm . . ." Lord Curzon to Mary Curzon, 31 July 1902, *Ibid.*, 118.

31. New Series, XIV, December 1984, 4.

32. *Ibid.*, 5.

33. Appropriately, after his retirement in 1938, the longtime Bahrain Political Agent Percy Loch achieved his cherished ambition and became Unicorn Pursuivant of Arms.

34. Compare Record, *Proud Century*, 80. See Rodney Dennys, *Heraldry and the Heralds,* Jonathan Cape, 1982, esp. Ch. 19, "Overseas Work of the Heralds".

35. G. A. Macaulay, *Schoolroom and Playing Field: A Centennial History of Timaru Boys' High School, 1880-1980*, Timaru Herald, Timaru, 1980, 26.

36. *Melioraora Sequamur, Brighton Grammar School, 1882-1982*, H. L. Hall, Brighton Grammar School, Brighton (Australia), 1983, 14.

37. Bruce Mansfield, *Knox: A History of Knox Grammar School, 1924-1974*, Knox Grammar School, Sydney (Australia), 1974, 114.

38. See IOR: L/P&S/15/35.

39. Mangan, *Athleticism*, 38.

40. Simon Jenkins, *The Companion Guide to Outer London*, Collins, 1981, 51.

78

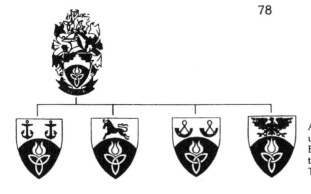

A 'Heraldic Educational Family', Ingeni use by the South African Department o Education and provincial departments the Cape, Natal, Orange Free State, an Transvaal.

41. "The contribution of Radleians to politics, business and commerce, sport, literature and the many other sides of our national life is frequently reported but their impact on Asia is perhaps less well known. It is therefore interesting to note the existence of an oriental association, founded nine years ago and now boasting almost one thousand members, which has Radleians as President, Secretary, Treasurer and member of Council . . . The association with which they are involved is known as 'B.A.C.A.', the British Association for Cemeteries in South Asia which was formed to preserve, convert and record old European cemeteries . . . Local projects have been developed in India, Pakistan, Bangladesh, Burma, Sri Lanka, Malaysia, etc., and an archive is being built up of biographical details in the India Office Library and Records." "Radley in Asia", *The Radleian*, 1985, 68.

42. *Ibid.*

43. Record, *Proud Century*, 300.

44. Mary Curzon, "Persian Gulf Journal", qtd. Bradley, *Lady Curzon's India*, 149.

45. King remarked: "Not all schools adopt one, but it is interesting to note that the general improvement of status in all kinds of non-grammar secondary school was generally contemporary with the adoption of a school uniform." He added: ". . . the fostering of *esprit de corps* by this method has also been associated with the spirit of the 'old school tie'." King, *Other Schools and Ours*, 226.

46. Record, *Proud Century*, 300-01. "It was also laid down that if sweaters bore Association Colours the order, beginning from the top, should be light blue, black, gold, black, light blue." *Ibid.*

47. James Laver, *The Book of Public School Old Boys,*

Radley. Its founder wrote in 1872, "One of the many uses of our public schools is to confer an aristocracy on boys who do not inherit it."

University, Navy, Army, Air Force & Club Ties, Seeley, 1968, 50. "The mere act of wearing a diagonally striped tie or a tie with some form of heraldic device . . . is a statement. The wearer is making a public claim to membership of the greater OBN. He is also claiming membership of a much smaller network within the OBN. If he is wearing blue and black he is telling you he is an Old Etonian; red, chocolate and blue—like Charles Ryder in the televised *Brideshead Revisited* that he is a Wykehamist (a rare liberty with Waugh's text); black or midnight blue with a double white stripe that he is an Harrovian; green, blue and white that he was at Rugby; pink and red on a dark ground indicates Charterhouse . . . no one except Britain has turned the necktie into such a precise form of communication." Tim Heald, *Networks*, Hodder and Stoughton, 1983, 21-22.

The author bought an Old Tonbridgian *bow* tie in London during the summer of 1985. The sales lady apologised for stocking them and said, "Some old boys wear them when they go to *America*."

48. Laver, *Book of . . . Ties*, 23, 66.

49. *Ibid.*, 31. "The general use of the old school tie began in the 1890s when many Old Boys' Associations were formed, followed a few years later by the introduction of a tie, often but not invariably adapted from the school colours." *Ibid.*

50. *Ibid.*, 28.

51. *Ibid.*, 30.

52. *Ibid*, 27.

53. Daily dress was scarcely less impressive. Political Agents in the Persian Gulf had six different uniforms, and a cocked hat with feathers that one former Agent described as "leaving a trail as if one were moulting". Arnold Galloway to P. J. Rich, 4 September 1987.

80

| Sovereign Commander of the Temple 27° A&A Rite | Sov Gd Commander A&A Rite for England & Wales | Sov Gd Commander A&AS Rite USA | Masonic Signatures. Some Masonic dignitaries sign their names with an accompanying flourish of nominals and crosses. |

54. *The Ampleforth Journal*, Winter 1984, Vol. LXXXIX, Part II, 31-32.

55. "Here the games ethic flourished, here was enthusiastic allegiance, here were housed the embryonic diffusionists and here a seductive image of Empire was projected unremittingly." Mangan, *The Games Ethic*, 43.

The Chapel of St.Mary Magdalen, Kingston upon Thames. An example of the integration of traditions. The chapel was established in 1305 by Edward Lovekyn, whose son was Lord Mayor of London. Subsequently donated by Queen Elizabeth I for use as Kingston Grammar School, it has been used for Masonic meetings. But Lovekyn Chantry Lodge for the old boys now meets in another part of the school which is heated!

CHAPTER FOUR

IMPERIAL FREEMASONRY

An English lodge is still to be found on every continent, and most possess many. Of course, the spread of English, Irish and Scottish masonry was largely the result of British colonialism, and in particular the vast expansion of the British Empire in the nineteenth century. While this Empire has now vanished, many of the lodges have remained.
K. W. Henderson, *Masonic World Guide,* 1984.

At the same time that the public schools were expanding their Imperial role, British freemasonry was undergoing unprecedented changes. Public school boys became the dominant force in the lodges, and Imperial leaders climbed the masonic and government ladders at the same time.[1]

It was the public schools that were "the breeding grounds of the masons of the late Victorian era".[2] So popular did joining the fraternity become that some schools had more than one lodge. Christ's Hospital supported *three* 'blue' lodges (lodges giving the first three degrees). Its Aldersgate Lodge No. 1657 was started in 1877 and the first initiate was the headmaster, Richard Lee. The other two were Christ's Hospital Lodge No. 2650, and Votum Lodge No. 6517. The school also had lodges giving the more advanced degrees, including a Mark Masters' Lodge, a Rose Croix Chapter, and a Royal Arch Chapter.[3]

Whatever else may be said about freemasonry, it was

82

Four Lewises, 1917. Young relatives of Freemasons, Lewises looked forward to joining the lodge at the age of eighteen rather than the statutory twenty-one. Here they carry the Sacred Law in a Provincial Grand Lodge of Corwall procession.

preoccupied with ritualism. In fact, it has been vigorously opposed on the grounds that it actually is a religion.[4] It exacted the same kind of passionate loyalty that the schools did.

Therefore it is not surprising that much of the criticism of freemasonry and public schools was similar. They were both accused of luxuriating in their exclusivity and of having members who were ". . . incapable of making rewarding social contacts except within a group where they can share in the experiences of a dramatic ritual."[5]

Twenty-six Royals

There were several reasons for the popularity of such a secret society. For one thing, it consistently enjoyed royal participation, which would have made membership attractive to ambitious Imperial administrators. It was a place where junior men could informally meet those of great position. At least twenty-six members of the Royal Family were members.[6]

Masonry also offered the inducement of awards that were outside the state honours system but equally coveted.[7] Extravagant titles were its stock-in-trade. It was possible to become a Sublime Knight Elect, Grand Master Architect, and Sovereign Prince of Rose Croix. More important, however, was the unique opportunity that it offered as the ultimate old boy network.[8] The famous old boy connection was cemented even more securely when someone was an old boy brother.

Headmasters as Brethren

So it is hardly startling to discover that many famous headmasters were active freemasons. H. B. Gray, Headmaster of Bradfield 1881-1910, was a member of Old Bradfieldian Lodge No. 3549. Harold Costley-White, Gray's successor as the Bradfield headmaster (1910-19) and then

83

Freemasons Hall, Dublin. Nearby is Trinity College, where Masonic meetings have been held since 1688.

headmaster of Westminster (1919-38), and Eric Whitworth, headmaster of Bradfield 1929-39 and headmaster of Tonbridge 1939-49 were initiated in Bradfield lodge. Costley-White became Grand Chaplain of the Grand Lodge. Another Bradfield lodge member was T. E. Wilson, headmaster of Ardingly 1915-32.[9] This involvement of leading headmasters is typical of the school lodges.

The Harrow School lodge boasted that two Headmasters had been initiated: Dr. Cyril Norwood in June 1931, and ten years later Mr. A. P. Boissier. The pattern continued: "Worshipful Brother R.L.James became a Joining Member on his appointment as Headmaster in 1953, and he twice served as Master of the Lodge."[10]

Through such associations, the rituals of school life became incorporated in the lodge rituals. The Headmaster became a Worshipful Master on certain evenings. The governing boards favoured this. The Provost and Chapter of Lancing presented the old boy lodge with the original bible used in Lancing Chapel since 1857, to be used in obligating candidates. Stones from the Chapel were used as ashlars[11] by the lodge in its ritual work.

The use by the lodges of school arms provide an example of the approval of the school, and illustrates as well the transfer of totems from the school to the lodge. Harrow's lodge for example had permission to use the school arms.[12] Another of many similar instances was Merchant Taylors' lodge:

> At a meeting of the Court of the Merchant Taylor's Company held on the 20th May 1879, it is minuted that 'There was read a letter, dated 26th ultimo, from the Reverend R. F. Hosken, one of the masters of the School, that a lodge of Freemasons is about to be formed consisting of past and present members of the School, to be called 'The Sir Thomas White Lodge' and asking permission to

Jewels of the Masonic Orders of Knight of Constantinople and Grand Tilers of Solomon. A variant working of Constantinople is now confined to Plymouth in England, but was worked in Hong Kong (1866) and Gibraltar (1868).

Musical Play, Haileybury, c.1900. Haileybury was no exception to the rapid development of public school drama in the later Victorian era, another way in which theatrical poise became part of the public school cachet. At the same time, costuming and staging of Masonic degrees was becoming more elaborate. Founded in 1862, the school displayed winged hearts and open book until joining with Imperial Service College and adding that school's motto, anchor, and sword. (left.)

Native Dancers greeting HMS Renown, Bushire, Arabian Gulf, 1 December 1921. Bushire was the headquarters for the British Political Agent, the so-called "Uncrowned King" of the Gulf. Visits of the Imperial navy created understudied port cultures which included stereotyped entertainments – urchins diving for coins, music and dancing even if there were no indigenous tradition – and left genetic legacies which belie ideas of cultural independence.
Masonic lodges in the Gulf depended for strength on military and civil service members.

use the Company's Arms upon the insignia of the lodge . . . it is resolved that the application be complied with."[13]

Creating Ritual

In the Victorian and Edwardian eras, the Empire, the schools and the lodges were industriously occupied with *creating* rituals.[14] Significantly, the schools began staging elaborate theatricals. (See *Musical Play, Haileybury,* page 85.) These were far more extravagant than the usual school productions, and deserve much more notice than they have so far received. The performers are a reminder that school ritualism had an anthropological significance that was never far from the surface. (See *Native Dancers, Greeting HMS Renown, Bushire, Arabian Gulf, 1 December 1921,* page 86.)

Both the schools and lodges went to considerable pains to give the impression that they were *conserving* rituals, not making them up. Ingenious apologetics enabled the innovations to appear as time-honoured traditions.[15] Even so, it was a time of costumed pageantry that seems to have been translated into Imperial pomp.

The new orders of the Empire found their counterparts in the new masonic lodges. London's Star of India lodge, to which Harrow's Welldon belonged, awarded its members a breast jewel resembling the Order of the Star of India.[16] There is considerable significance to the use of an Imperial order by people who had not been awarded it. It should be added that Welldon belonged as well to Lodge Himalayan Brotherhood in India,[17] and joined the Eton and Harrow old boy lodges. He was chaplain of the Harrow lodge in 1924.[18]

87

British Postage Stamp. Trowel and square and compass can be clearly seen. King George VI was an enthusiastic Grand Master and Grand Patron.

Reinforcing Imperialism

For an Imperialist such as Welldon, the lodges were an important meeting ground.[19] Present, in 1897, at an Empire Lodge London dinner, were the Earl of Lathorn, Lord Saltoun, the Duke of Abercorn, the Raja of Kapurthala, and the Premiers of Natal, New South Wales, Victoria, Tasmania, and New Zealand. The same year, Empire initiated the Raja of Khetri and the son of the Raja of Shahpura and in 1906 the Sultan of Jahore, and fifteen years later, his son. In 1928 the lodge secretary travelled 65,000 miles visiting members.[20]

The ways in which freemasonry was involved in Imperial administration are difficult to research because of its secrecy: "Its role in spreading British cultural influences has thus been seriously underrated."[21] What is clear is that lodge administration began to emulate Imperial administration. British masonic bodies insisted on their right to govern masonic affairs in overseas territories and adopted titles indicating this. The masonic order became imperial at the same time as British government.

There were those who thought that a secret society such as freemasonry could help to reinforce Imperial hegemony. One of these was Cecil Rhodes, who was a freemason but after considering "using" the masons moved towards the idea of forming a new secret society "to devote itself to the preservation and expansion of the British Empire."[22] Of course secrecy itself has many uses, but along with secrecy there was the ritualism. It was the ritualism as much or more than the secrecy that helped to enforce rule, clothing the Imperial authority with awe-inspiring rites.[23] It was all the better to have some of them mysterious.

Lodges were started in many parts of the Empire, and amazingly soon after the first rudimentary British presence had been achieved. Lagos Lodge No. 1171 of the English Grand Lodge was started in 1867.[24] Sometimes members took the lodge with them when they emigrated—freemasonry in South Australia started with consecration of Lodge of Friendship No. 613 in London in 1834. The lodge then

88

Brockton High School, Canada. This example of Canadian school heraldry was collected by Professor Ian Campbell of the University of Waterloo.

emigrated to Adelaide in 1838.[25] As the Empire retreated, the lodge would be returned to Britain, for example Caledonian Lodge of Uganda No. 1389, which now meets in Edinburgh.[26]

The Ultimate Cabal

What was created with the worldwide expansion of freemasonry was the ultimate old boy cabal. More than 170 lodges were formed at schools and for old boys of particular schools. Notices of masonic meetings began to appear in school magazines, in sharp contrast with the usual masonic reticence about publicity. Overseas public schools were no exception to this, and the connection persisted well into the twentieth century. This is illustrated by an item in the Australian *Old Melburnians*:

> Old Melburnians Lodge with its 90 members is just one cog in an organisation of 6 million members throughout the world with 70,000 in Victoria . . . we offer our congratulations to the Right Worshipful Brother the Honourable Mr. Justice Austin Asche Grand Master, who was installed as Grand Master of the United Grand Lodge of Victoria in March 1984. He is an Old Boy of the School (1934 to 1943) and a member of our Lodge.[27]

In fact, Australian schools had just as many lodges connected with them as English schools did. The number that can be identified in Victoria alone is astonishing, and the list is by no means complete: Mt. Scopus Collegians No. 827, Burwood; Ivanhoe Grammarians No. 584, Darebin; Malvern Grammarians No. 693, Glenferrie; Scotch Collegians No. 396, Glenferrie; Carey Grammarians No. 810, Kew; Trinity Grammarians No. 500, Kew; Camberwell Grammar No. 615, Glenferrie; University High School No. 517, Kew; Old Melburnians No. 317, Prahran; Melbourne High School No.

Britannia School. Professor Campbell's survey of Canadian school heraldry demonstrates that Masonic symbolism was uncommon but not unknown.

759; Wesley Collegians' No.358, Prahran; Caulfield Grammarians No. 364, St. Kilda.[28]

The existence of so many school lodges is almost an argument that to be accepted as fully a public school it was essential to have a masonic lodge. An historian of Prince Alfred College in Adelaide recounted what is a pro-typical story of the founding of a public school lodge:

> Towards the end of 1907 about thirty old boys who were members of the Order of Freemasons, after due deliberation, founded the Prince Alfred Collegians' Lodge. It was No. 51 on the roll of the Grand Lodge of South Australia, and was the first of the 'College' Lodges in this State. It was followed very quickly by a similar Lodge formed by the old boys of St. Peter's College . . . The first new member to be elected and initiated into the rites of Freemasonry in the new Lodge was the veteran Headmaster, Mr. Chapple.[29]

The Festival

The big event in public school freemasonry was the annual festival, when masons from all over England and overseas descended on a particular school for an orgy of ritualism. These festivals have continued in the post World War II era and in fact have gathered strength.[30]

The festival was usually commemorated by an elaborate souvenir programme published by the host lodge, complete with an account of the host school's masonic activities. Glowing remarks were made about the masonic accomplishments of old boys, after suitably modest apologies for the boasting. The Master of the Old Alleynian Lodge remarked at a Dulwich festival: "I am going so far to depart from the rule that I have set myself of not mentioning the names of Old Alleynians as to refer to two, and this for a special reason in each case. The first is Sir Ernest

90

The Ninth Degree. The Elu or Elect of Nine is in a series of so-called High Grades, eighteenth century in origin, and connected with the House of Stuart, hermeticism and magism.

Shackleton, because he was a Founder of this Lodge, and the other is (Brother) Stainforth, because he holds the unique record of having travelled at a faster speed than any human being."[31]

Grand Wardens and Grand Deacons

Many Imperial administrators would not join their school lodge because they were not able to attend. They preferred to join a lodge where they were stationed. On the other hand, a surprisingly large number did affiliate with an old boys' lodge. These school lodges were remarkably well represented in the higher reaches of masonic and Imperial leadership. Typically, one of the active brothers in the Old Tonbridgian Lodge was the Assistant Grand Director of Ceremonies of the English Grand Lodge, Sir Maurice Simpson, who also headed communications for the India Office as Director-in-Chief of the Indo-European telegraph service. Symptomatic of the umbilical old boyism that influenced the Empire, he always led his list of various distinctions in *Who's Who* with: *Tonbridge School, Head boy, 1885.*[32]

The Old Westminsters' Lodge included the Deputy Grand Master for India's masonic province of Madras, Sir Archibald Campbell. Another Old Westminster became Grand Deacon of the Grand Lodge, Sir Arthur Knapp. At the same time that he was Grand Deacon, he was Member and Vice President of the Executive Council for Madras. His masonic brother and fellow O.W., Campbell, was Member of the Board of Revenue. Knapp became a Governor of Westminster and Campbell became Chief Secretary of the Madras Government (1925-30) while he was serving as Deputy Grand Master.

Despite the difficulties that distance entailed, all the old boy lodges had members like Knapp and Campbell who were high-ranking officers of the order overseas. The Charterhouse Lodge boasted the past Deputy Grand Masters for both the Bombay province and Bengal. The Old Shirburnian Lodge included the Senior Grand Warden of the Grand Lodge, Field

Royal Arch Chapter, Bangkok. Often associated with a particular lodge, Royal Arch chapters confer further degrees that have their own symbolism. See page 128.

Marshal Sir Claud Jacob. At the same time he was Secretary of the Military Department of the India Office, having previously (1920-24) been Chief of the General Staff in India.

In the old boy lodges, as already noted, it was probable that one would encounter headmasters and masters. There they mixed with Imperial officials. The Old Cliftonian Lodge included a headmaster both of Clifton and Rugby and past Grand Chaplain of the Grand Lodge, the Bishop of Liverpool, A. A. David. A fellow member was the past Senior District Grand Warden for East Africa, Sir Charles Bowring, who was Chief Secretary for Kenya (1911-24) and Governor of Nyasaland (1924-29), and was at the same time a Grand Deacon of the Grand Lodge.

The Old Wellingtonian lodge, besides having the Grand Master of all English masons (The Duke of Connnaught), included in its membership the Provincial Grand Master for Lancashire, The Earl of Derby. The Treasurer of the Grand Lodge belonged to the Old Marlburian Lodge, as did the Grand Organist. The Old Rugbeian Lodge included Sir Walter Napier, who was District Grand Master of the Eastern Archipelago. The Old Haileyburian Lodge's most prominent member was the doyen of Middle East freemasons, Right Worshipful Brother Gen. Sir A. Henry McMahon, GCMG, GCVO, KCIE, CSI. He was Past Grand Warden of the Grand Lodge, and Deputy Provincial Grand Master for Malta.

As might be expected, the Old Etonian lodge was overwhelmed with Grand Lodge officers, including the Earl of Yarborough, the Earl of Shaftesbury, Lord Cornwallis, the Duke of Devonshire, Lord Kensington, the Earl of Harewood, and Lord Hailsham. Old Harrovians had fewer peers in Grand Lodge office than the Etonians, but included Lord Lilford, Lord Forester, and Lord Tomlin of Ash.[33]

The Magic Circle

Undoubtedly there were many reasons why prominent men became freemasons, but one thing that they found appealing

92

The Point within a Circle. Concededly among the most puzzling of Masonic symbols, it has phallic and magical connotations.

was its ritual. Evidence of this, for those who are puzzled as to what induced so many well known individuals to spend time and money on freemasonry, can be found in Rudyard Kipling's work. The connection between Imperialism and freemasonry is substantiated and celebrated by much of what Kipling wrote.

What comes across strongly in Kipling's work, if one knows where to look, is the appeal of a magic circle, a brotherhood united by esoteric ceremonialism. Masonic themes and expressions can be found in such stories of his as *On the Great Wall, The Winged Hat, Hal o' the Draft*, and *The City Wall*. His most famous masonic story is of course *The Man Who Would Be King*.

In the original edition of the *Just So Stories*, the drawing done by his father to accompany *The Butterfly That Stamped* pictures King Solomon adorned with a masonic apron, sash, and emblem. Besides the stories, some of his poems may be positively labelled 'Masonic'. Among them are *The Palace, Banquet Night, The Widow of Windsor, Rough Ashlar* and *Mother Lodge*.[34]

Besides this literary evidence he gave of his interest, he helped to found two lodges: Authors' Lodge No.3456 and Builders of the Silent Cities No. 4948. Moreover, he was poet laureate of the famous Edinburgh lodge, Cannongate-Kilwinning. One predecessor in that office was Robert Burns.[35]

Some Practical Reasons

The Imperial interest in masonry was not just ritualistic. There were practical reasons why a boy planning to spend a lifetime in Imperial service would consider joining a lodge. The masons had an effective system of communications and hospitality. Membership meant admission to the elite in any of Britain's colonies.[36] For the same rather basic reasons, on becoming headmaster a man was expected to take an interest in masonry.[37]

93

The Count of Cagliostro (1743-1795). Becoming a Mason in 1776 in Esperance Lodge in London and castigated as charlatan, he envisaged Freemasonry undermining political tyranny. His Egyptian Rite influenced nineteenth-century British Masonry.

All of which explains why, if there is no public school *cum* masonic "conspiracy", it is still necessary to deal with the perception created by such activities. Recently (1988) in England the controversy over masonic involvement in politics has flared again, with *The Independent* newspaper conducting a campaign against police membership in the order. If the issue is not a closed one in England, neither is it of only academic interest abroad.

Overseas masonry, royalty's connection with masonry, and the desire of old boys to have their own lodges, are not extinct forces. In April 1986 the notice of the Supreme Grand Chapter of Royal Arch Masons of England, a body conferring some of the higher degrees that is headed by HRH The Duke of Kent, listed petitions for a chapter to be attached to the Enfield School Lodge, No. 7757 and for a chapter to meet at the Masonic Temple, Kitwe, Zambia.[38]

Interesting as it may be that such activities persist, in the past the connections were much more far-reaching. The old boy freemason was the archetype of the Imperial ritualist. His native pupils in the former Empire yielded to no one in their bemedalled glory. (See *Rt. Wor. Bro. His Highness Sir Raza Ali Khan Bahadur, Nawab of Rampur, President Masonic Fraternity of New Delhi,* page 95.) Other results of this extreme devotion to ritualism were less dazzling but more serious, as will be seen.

Eighteenth-century Apron. Freemasonry and heraldry were plagued by the pseudo-antiquarian legacy of shadowy figures such as Cagliostro. In Masonry's case, sometimes sole surviving authentic evidence of early symbolism is an apron.

Rt.Wor.Bro.His Highness Sir Raza Ali Khan
Bahadur, Nawab of Rampur, President Masonic
Fraternity of New Delhi. Not only medals but
aprons come in a bewildering variety of styles.
Perhaps Masonry provided a substitute for
"real" orders like the Royal Victorian and
British Empire.

ROYAL VICTORIAN · BRITISH EMPIRE

NOTES—CHAPTER FOUR

1. See K. W. Henderson, *Masonic World Guide*, Lewis Masonic, 1984, esp. 94-95.

2. A. C. F. Jackson, "Our Predecessors of about the time that Quator Coronati Lodge was founded", *Ars Quatuor Coronatorum*, Vol. 90, 1977, 41.

3. Some freemasons take exception to describing additional degrees as "higher" or "advanced", claiming that they merely elucidate on the masonic message rather than actually conferring a more exalted status.

4. See *Freemasonry: Is it a Religion?* Church Literature Association, 1986.

5. James Dewar, *The Unlocked Secret: Freemasonry Examined*, William Kimber, 1986, 233. ". . . the pleasure of secret rites, challenging ordeals, and a group . . . Adolescents, in particular, often join such secret groups . . . they are especially open to the allure of secret societies . . . It marks their acceptance into a community of those who *can* keep secrets, and who have important secrets to keep." Sissela Bok, *Secrets: On the Ethics of Concealment and Revelation*, Oxford University Press, 1986, 48-49.

6. Audrey Whiting, *The Kents*, Futura, 1985, 178.

7. See Henry L. Hall "Orders (Fleece-Star-Garter)", *The New*

Grand Lodge of Israel. The design includes symbols of three major religions, enclosed by the square and compass. Israel's lodges, some dating back to the British occupation, work in Hebrew, Turkish, French, English, Spanish, Arabic and German.

Age, published by The Supreme Council, 33°, Southern Jurisdiction, Vol. XCV, No. 1, January 1987, 39-43.

8. Mary Kenny, "Masonic Rites and Wrongs", *The Sunday Telegraph*, 5 April 1987, 21. ". . . the Club can help you with careers much the same way as the Freemasons. If your boss is also an O.O. you will go far . . . one of the most respected and envied Old Boy Networks." *The Laxtonian, Oundle School Magazine, 1986*, 17.

9. G. Norman Knight, *Old Bradfieldian Lodge No. 3549, Historical Notes*, Old Bradfieldian Lodge. Most of the following lodge histories were published by the lodge itself. They can all be found in the library of the United Grand Lodge of England, London. The bibliographical details are based on somewhat eccentric titling.

10. *44th Festival of the Public School Lodges at Harrow School, 28 May 1977*. A year after the founding of Old Epsomian Lodge, the headmaster, T. W. H. Smith-Pearse was initiated (1912). R. D. Hyem, *Historical Notes for Jubilee Celebration, Old Epsomian Lodge No. 3561*, 1961, Old Epsomian Lodge. At Merchant Taylors', members besides assistant masters included the school secretary, chaplain, and two headmasters, Dr. Nairn and Brian Reeves. *Festival of the Public School Lodges at Merchant Taylors'* The founding master of Old St. Edward's Lodge was Bishop Southwell, Chairman of the School Governors, and the lodge notices appeared in the school's magazine. *25th Festival of the Public Schools Lodge Council*, Old St. Edward's Lodge No. 5162, 31 May 1958.

11. Most school lodge publications made extensive use of the school colours and evidently the same can be said of the appointments in the lodge apartments.

12. "On February 22, 1932, the lodge received permission from the Governors to use the Arms and Badge of the School." *History and Bye-Laws, Old Harrovian Lodge No. 4653*.

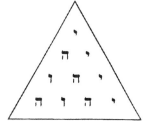

The tetragrammaton. The device occurs in Masonic literature about the Ineffable Name used in rites such as the Cryptic and Ark of Enoch. Arranging the letters permits manifesting the 72 powers of deity.

13. *Festival of the Public School Lodges at Merchant Taylors'*, 9 June 1979.

14. The officers involved in creating Imperial rituals were sometimes the same as those involved in implementing masonic rituals. The Richmond Herald was Director of Ceremonies of Old Harrovian lodge. *History and Bye-Laws, Old Harrovian Lodge*. Sir Gerald Wollaston, Garter King at Arms and member of Old Harrovian lodge, presided over the masonic festival at Eton in 1935. *The Nineteenth Public Schools Masonic Festival at Eton College, June 15, 1935*. The Band of the Royal Horse Guards played and the headmaster of Eton, C. A. Elliott, hosted in full masonic regalia.

15. It should be added in fairness that there has been a considerable movement in masonry to "de-mythogize" the fraternity's history and acknowledge that much of the ritual is of comparatively recent origin.

16. *Star of India Lodge No. 3444, A Review from the Consecration to the Fiftieth Anniversary.*

17. G. Reeves-Brown, ed., *Extracts from the Minutes, Lodge Himalayan Brotherhood*, Rev. Ed. (E. O. Wiley, ed.), Simla, 1927.

18. *History and Bye-Laws, Old Harrovian Lodge No.4653.*

19. See, for example, *A History of the Empire Lodge No. 2108, Consecrated 24th November 1885*, rev. 1977.

20. *Ibid.*

21. Ronald Hyam, *Britain's Imperial Century, 1815-1914: A Study of Empire and Expansion*, B&N, 1976, 152-53. Compare John Chandos, *Boys Together: English Public Schools 1800-1864*, Oxford University Press, 1985, 20. John A. Armstrong,

98

CIA Composite Club. A device of a Central Intelligence Agency secret group of Freemasons, one of several: the 'Royal Craft' continues as shaman's lair for apparachiks.

The European Administrative Elite, Princeton University Press (New Jersey), 1973, 234.

22. Carroll Quigley, *The Anglo-American Establishment: From Rhodes to Cliveden*, Books in Focus, New York, 1981, ix, 39.

23. ". . . those who are to enjoy pre-eminence or to exercise power, should be invested with some ideal influence which may serve to clothe the nakedness of authority." Sir Henry Taylor, "The Rationale of Linking High Office to High Status", W. L. Guttsman, ed. *The English Ruling Class*, Weidenfeld and Nicolson, 1969, 230. See Hyam, *Britain's Imperial Century*, 153.

24. Henderson, *Masonic World Guide*, 57. See *Ibid.*, 151, 162, 163.

25. *Ibid.*, 332.

26. *Regular Lodges Masonic*, Bloomington (Illinois), 1984, 236. This is evidently a book issued to tylers of lodges to determine if a visitor came from a recognized lodge.

27. *The Old Melburnians*, No. 23, May 1984, 3.

28. *Regular Lodges, passim*.

29. J. F. Ward, *Prince Alfred College: The story of the first eighty years, 1869-1949*, Prince Alfred College, Adelaide (Australia), 1951, 130.

30. *Old Tonbridgian Lodge No. 4145, 1920-1970*, Programme, 37th Festival of the Public School Lodges Council at Tonbridge School, 9th May 1970, 20.

31. *A Short Address on the History of the College delivered by The Worshipful Master of the Old Alleynian Lodge No. 4165 at the Sixteenth Festival of the Public School Lodges*, 11 June 1932, 11.

The Pythagorean Signet Ring and Five Pointed Star. Sometimes associated with the 28th degree, Knight of the Sun.

32. *Who Was Who*, Vol. V, 1951-1960, 1003.

33. For the preceding affiliations with the old boy lodges see *Public Schools Masonic Year Book*, revised to 31st July 1930, np, 13-18.

34. See *Kipling*, Masonic Service Association, Silver Spring (Maryland), 1964.

35. *Ibid.*

36. See Hyam, *Imperial Century*, 152-53.

37. Tim Heald, *Networks: Who We Know and How We Use Them*, Hodder and Stoughton, 1983, 183.

38. *Supreme Grand Chapter Notice*, 18 April 1986, 4.

Great Seal of the United States of America. Masonic influence seen in the all-seeing eye and incomplete pyramid, as well as in the alteration of the Latin motto from *Saeclorum*.

CHAPTER FIVE

THE CONSEQUENCES OF RITUALISM

*Oh yes, it is a real public school. I mean, they don't
learn anything there.*
A Lady, quoted by Archbishop Temple.

As has been seen, boys learned a great deal indeed about
ritual in their public school.[1] They went out into the world
with that knowledge, and with a supreme self-confidence that
had much to do with the Empire's success. Their position as
British administrators was reinforced by the same kind of
legerdemain which had enabled them as prefects to run their
houses without adult help.[2]

The scrupulously enforced ritualism in schools may on
occasion have produced some pathologically frustrated
individuals: self-expression was repressed. In the Empire, the
same repressive attitudes may have hastened the demise of
indigenous cultures.

The British seldom displayed any qualms about interjecting
their views about every topic under the colonial sun. When it
came to education, they imposed their notions of schooling
with what was at times an unpleasant authoritarianism.[3] Their
education gave them what Said called 'a positional
superiority',[4] enabling them *always* to have the upper hand
in their relationships with the local population. Their audience
was a captive one.

That the British could visit or live in a foreign country by
right, while the natives came to England only as *invited*

101

Sydney Grammar School. Granted by the Kings of
Arms in 1951. One of Australia's "Great Public
Schools", an Australian term comparable to the
Clarendon Schools' designation of top
British institutions.

guests after receiving *permission*, made the relationships one-sided from the start. Lacking consular representation and prevented by treaty from contact with other governments, the local peoples had to supplicate for the simplest favours such as travel papers. They were reduced to being simply junior boys who had to ask the prefect if they could go into town.

Creating Insecurity

The ritualistic paraphernalia of Empire contributed to the insecurity felt by colonial subjects, who were always being put off balance by coming to the dinner party in the wrong clothes. The Empire's administrators, for their part, were possessed of monumental *sang froid*.[5] Much of the public schoolboy's success depended on the way his ritualistic behaviour produced this lack of confidence and almost paranoic self-criticism in the natives.[6]

A prime example of what the public schools wrought in the Empire was the spread of the presumptuous notion that education should be different for different social classes. This was reinforced through the schools' perpetuation of linguistic differences which helped to identify the classes—hence the phrase 'public school accent'.[7]

The native schools were often humble and poorly equipped. Nevertheless, it can be argued that in some cases a society's educational and social divisions were fewer before British Imperialism interfered. Muslims in particular stressed educational equality and seemed to have had an attitude analogous to the Welsh or Scottish position as far as general education was concerned. Elitism did exist in Arab society, but didn't enjoy the ascendancy it had acquired in England.

The Imperial onslaught profoundly influenced these attitudes. An illustration from the Arabian Gulf demonstrates the English influence at work. Gerald De Gaury, the Political Agent at Kuwait, wrote to the Political Resident, Trenchard Fowle, to dismiss the idea of general secondary schooling for Kuwaitis, stating that surely the instruction of "intelligent poor

102

Sydney Church of England Grammar School.
Another of the so-called Great Public Schools.
Granted by the Kings of Arms in 1932 and
incorporating a torch and escallop from unofficial
badges.

boys" would have to be vocational rather than "liberal". Fowle concurred.[8]

Administrators such as De Gaury and Fowle were the rule rather than the exception. They did not come by the view that the poor should be educated differently from the rich only when they were posted overseas. It was part of their baggage when they left England. Their attitudes were not acquired accidentally.[9]

Athleticism and Ritualism

Recent debate[10] over the public schools has centred on their function in the moulding of attitudes such as those expressed by De Gaury and Fowle.[11] Good or bad, this inculcation of hierarchicalism set the public schools apart from other kinds of secondary education. Explaining just how this was accomplished has been a daunting task.

As previously mentioned, J. A. Mangan has effectively called attention to the contribution of athleticism, a variant of muscular Christianity *cum* Imperialism. This was explored as well by David Newsome in *Godliness and Good Learning*. The popular effect of such studies has been to substitute an image of the games cult, exemplified by hearty old boy missionaries and Indian versions of Eton, for previous vagaries invoking Dr. Arnold.

Although it has been a recent focus of scholars, athleticism really upon further consideration is a manifestation rather than an explanation of the public schools. It does not fully explain how public schoolism provided so much support for British cultural hegemony. Interesting as it is as a social study, athleticism does not explain why the schools had such importance. The ritualistic life of the schools does. In the triumph of public school hegemony, athleticism was an ingredient. It was rivalled or surpassed by the chapel, the masonic lodge, and other institutions whose common denominator is ritualism.

Indoctrination in ritualism was more important than

Heraldry Society of Australia. Again a Southern Cross design.

academic success. The logistics of Imperial ritualism could be enormous. The careful training in public school or in a masonic lodge was a preparation for grander efforts. (See *Lodge of Freemasons*, Page 105.) Once the tests of school and masonry had been passed, it was possible to face larger ceremonies with equanimity. The Coronation Durbar in Delhi in 1902 required the efforts of several hundred thousand men. (See *The Delhi Coronation Durbar*, Page 106.)

In fact, the British overseas did not judge native education by scholastic success, because they did not judge themselves by that criterion. It was sometimes the academic success that was trivial to them, not the ritualism. When their colonial subjects won academic laurels, they suspected that the accomplishment was superficial, achieved without absorbing the real lessons that the schools taught.[12]

The subtlety of public school ritualism complicated the picture for native educators. They were confronted with the fact that what others might call *style* constituted *substance* to the old boys. The attention by overseas schools to colours and armorial bearings arose from hopes of capturing the secret of 'public schoolism'.

Anonymous Villains

The influence of the schools on the Empire, as well as of the Empire on the schools, was all the more complicated because it was so often an 'anonymous villain'.[13] In the case of public school freemasonry the anonymity was deliberate. The complicated ties between the Empire and the schools and lodges were taken as a matter of course, and not frequently questioned.

Examination of prospectuses however, reveals a pattern of tell-tale phrases ("The school specializes in the preparation of boys for the ICS.") that betray the close relationships. Undoubtedly there were further relationships that so far have

104

Princes of Jerusalem. Jewel of the 25th degree in the Ancient and Accepted Rite, with the initials of Darius and Zerubbabel.

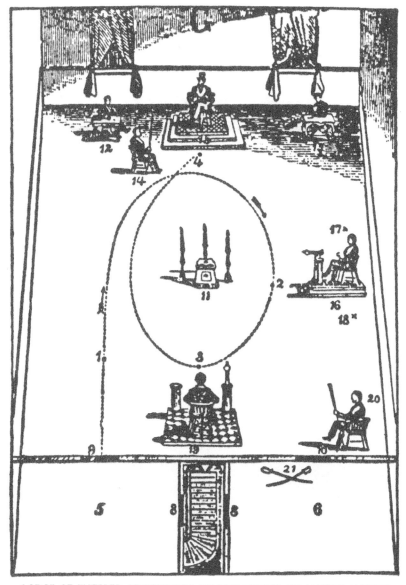

LODGE OF ENTERED APPRENTICES, FELLOW CRAFTS, OR MASTER MASONS.

1. Candidate prays. 2. First stop. 3. Second stop. 4. Third stop. 5. Room where candidates are prepared. 6. Ante-room where members enter the lodge. 7. Hall. 8. Doors. 9. Door through which candidates are admitted into the lodge. 10. Door through which members enter. 11. Altar. 12. Treasurer. 13. Secretary. 14. Senior Deacon. 15. Worshipful Master. 16. Junior Warden. 17 and 18. Stewards. 19. Senior Warden. 20. Junior Deacon. 21. Tyler.

Nineteenth-century lodge floor plan. Temple layouts in the Empire varied, usually according to Irish, Scottish, and English grand lodge antecedents. Each had its own floor work. Great Seal of the Grand Lodge of Scotland (right).

The Delhi Coronation Durbar, 1902. Opportunities to impress the natives were seized with enthusiasm: the 1911 Delhi Durbar was an occasion for distributing 200 gold and 30,000 silver medals. 1911 Medal (right).

gone undetected. There have lately been attempts to describe the schooling that was distinctive to different colonies, linking the school background of the administrators with the colony they served.[14] The Sudan is an example of a British possession that has had its civil service's school background extensively and interestingly studied, thanks to Mangan and Kirk-Greene.

Additional evidence of this somewhat subtle ideological contribution of the public schools to British life is the alternative schools that sprang up. Because public schools set such store on imparting values, educators were spurred to found alternative schools, rather as splinter religious sects emphasized one doctrine over another. The launching of new foundations in the nineteenth and twentieth centuries testifies as to how seriously educators took the schools' influence: seriously enough to start schools which would instil different values.[15]

Lasting Repercussions

The consequences of living a highly ritualistic life in an all-male community during the formative years of adolescence were immense. There should be no illusions about the psychological effects of the public school education. It was a traumatic experience that had repercussions throughout a boy's life.

Public schools aggressively shaped the personalities of the students who became colonial rulers. The indoctrination was as forceful as in Moral Re-armament or a Jesuit novitiate. Later, in their role as Platonic warders, the old boys energetically imposed the same ideas on the Imperial administration.[16]

This is *not* to deny that other forces contributed to the character of the Imperialist. Family and friends determine lifelong attitudes when the child lives at home, but it should

Lodge Polynesia, Fiji. A "homemade" but serviceable badge of a lodge visited by the author and dating from 1875. Located on Ovalau Island.

be remembered that they lose influence when the child boards. The time spent at school meant that home in some cases was relegated to a secondary place. In an interview in *The Tonbridgian*, Colin Cowdrey was asked, "How do you look back on your life at Tonbridge now?": "I came from India in 1938 . . . Tonbridge became the thing I clung to . . . I didn't see my family for seven years."[17]

Boarding represented an appealing option for children of parents living overseas, and for the children of the Empire's subject peoples aspiring to British acceptance. R. F. Delderfield limns them as 'sunsetters'. He wrote in *To Serve Them All My Days*: ". . . boys known as 'The Sunsetters', a group nickname . . . invented for the score or so boarders who lived permanently at the school because their parents were scattered about the dominions, the Crown colonies and the protectorates."[18] The term played on the claim that Britain ruled an empire on which the sun never set and was a good-natured joke about the separateness of boys who looked upon school as a home.

Pietism vs. Culturism

Distinctions drawn between school influence on the Empire and the general influence of British culture are redolent of the discussions by historians about drawing the line between educational and general history. This debate centres on the merits of *pietistic* approaches, the specific and institutional approach that has vied for attention with *culturism*.

Such fixed definitions of education restrict the historian's curiosity about relevant non-school activity such as the old boy lodges. There are other numerous examples of non-school educational influences which deserve consideration. When historians fond of culturism emphasize those non-school aspects such as family, it should be added that a family that profoundly believed in the public school would reinforce school values.

Thus, arguments for the family and other non-school in-

Monarchist League. A worldwide organization for those interested in monarchy as an effective means of government.

fluences can be turned around and used in favour of the importance of the school *culture*. Indeed, the public school influence resembles the family influence in its intensity. The public schools proclaimed their inclusive culture as a virtue and were proud about having an impact that went beyond the curriculum. In short, pietism and culturism both support the school's place in history.

While all the ways in which the schools affected British leadership in comparison with the leadership of other countries are not yet described, an indication of where inquiries might lead is provided by Judith Hughes in *Emotion and High Politics: Personal Relations at the Summit in Late Nineteenth-Century Britain and Germany*.[19] Hughes shows how the widening gap in understanding between Britain and Germany after 1880 partly resulted from the education and upbringing of the leaders.

The consequences of the public school system must be included in any consideration of British history in the nineteenth and twentieth centuries. In particular, it should be noted how the Empire became more and more ritualistic in its activities, just as the schools became more and more ritualistic in their activities.

In the Empire, every administrator became an educator in the sense that he was closely watched and copied. Admittedly if this were belaboured it would bring culturism in Imperial educational history to the borderline of anthropology, too general an hypothesis to be productive. Nevertheless, it remains true that much of educational influence was outside the classroom.

In the Spirit of Lighthouse Maintenance

No matter what is said about 'benign neglect' or 'indirect rule' in the Empire, as a matter of fact the British organized a fair amount of schooling wherever they went. Much of this was organized by them in the same routine spirit as they approached lighthouse maintenance and road renewal. For

Chief Herald of Ireland. The post dates only to the 1943 establishment of the Republic. The ancient office of Ulster King of Arms was united with that of Norroy King of Arms at the College in London.

making educational decisions they had no formal background. Therefore they relied on their own school experiences.

Even today, with the mushrooming of professionalism in education, the suspicion is that the adolescent experiences of those who make decisions is as likely to play a part in the "why" of their policies as later tertiary courses in John Dewey. Because the public school experience dominated the lives of those serving overseas, there inevitably will be further discoveries of its effects on the Empire.

The preceding argument is certainly not that the public schools were the *only* influence on Imperial decisions. It is an argument that the schools had a significant place alongside diplomatic, economic, and geopolitical forces. A historian of the Empire cannot ignore the ways in which education effected the organization and distribution of power. The direct and indirect exclusion of groups from education was as influential on Imperial development as the obvious political decisions. Education for leadership and the decision *not* to educate the majority of the population had profound consequences.

When it came to the Empire's elite civil services, public schoolism was a "mental gymnastic" which enabled officers to cope with a spectrum of problems without calling in specialists. This exaltation of the generalist over the specialist was reflected in the way British officials dealt on the same day with judicial, educational, medical, and military matters. The seeds of this confidence were in staring down town boys and lording over the smaller pupils. Thus was instilled the faith that the Empire could be run like a public school. The atmosphere of the schools produced a confidence in the rightness of things British and an imperturbability in the face of crises. Like an evangelical preacher, the public school-educated administrator believed that the locals welcomed his exhortations.[20]

To impose oneself on tribal chieftains and fierce bedouins, an overweening self-importance was not a bad qualification. Midst the tribal warfare and Great Power plotting that characterized the period, a public school background gave

110

Dr.William's School, Merioneth. A pile reversed sable ensigned on the top with a fire-beacon proper, on a chief of the second, three mullets of six points of the first.

the monumental unflinchingness needed to keep Britannia's enemies at bay. It was less successful in dealing with the increasing technological demands of the twentieth century.

The Other Side of the Flag

The inequity of the public school system was enormous. So was the inequity of the Empire, an inequity which continued right up until its end. The old school tie was the only one in the drawer. Those in search of social salvation without it received scant encouragement from the *Times Educational Supplement* (17 July 1947), which mused:

> The parent who can say "My son is at Puffington" has an advantage over a parent who has to say "My son is at the Main Street Secondary Modern School, Blanktown" . . . The Ministry of Education shows an exquisite appreciation of the difference by suggesting that school names should emphasize unity rather than diversity in the secondary system' and that therefore the term 'modern', 'grammar', 'technical' should be avoided, as well as the street name.

Blanktown never triumphed over Puffington, but cosmetics helped to conceal the gross inequalities. Unfortunately the problems created were more severe than a distribution of blazers could solve.

111

The Champion Annual, 1924. Natives quaked, but the British boy never lost his nerve.

NOTES—CHAPTER FIVE

1. "The expression of emotions is culturally learned, and after it has been learned biological consequences occur . . . institutions provide man with models for action, enabling him to speak, feel, and act in a taken-for-granted prereflective way . . . Most important of all, they provide his emotions with a framework that both *stabilizes* and *stimulates* them. We may therefore assert that human emotions are not only embedded in but also dependent upon social institutions." Anton C. Zijderveld, *The Abstract Society: A Cultural Analysis of Our Time*, Penguin Books, Harmondsworth, 1974, 144-45.

2. See *Ibid.*, 220.

3. ". . . because of the institutions, we can expect typical role behaviour on the part of others, who expect the same from us. These expectations, having an 'objective' ground in the institutional structure, possess the power to coerce our behaviour into certain established patterns. This enhances the predictability of our actions." *Ibid.*, 145.

4. Said, *Orientalism*, 7.

5. For incidents of this, told tongue-in-cheek, see Philip Mason, *A Shaft of Sunlight*, Andre Deutsch, 1978, *passim.*

6. Allen, *Plain Tales*, 261.

7. See W. F. Bolton, *The Language of 1984*, Blackwell, Oxford, 83.

Empress of India Medal, 1877. Commemorating the proclamation of Queen Victoria as Empress and awarded in both gold and silver.

8. IOR: "Kuwait Education", R/15/5/195, 59. Fowle cautioned De Gaury that: ". . . we should not be educating the boys beyond a station to which they could not hope to obtain." *Ibid.*

9. Not only were such attitudes part of the hidden curriculm of English schools, but also they were the *reason* for overseas schools. See, for example, *Bulletin*, Wanganui Collegiate School (New Zealand), August 1985, No. 8, 10.

10. See *Woodbridge School: An Outline History*, Eric Ayres, Ipswich, 1962, 4.

11. See Morris, *Pax Britannica*, 140.

12. *Ibid.*

13. Derek Verschoyle, the book reviewer and *Spectator* columnist, was convinced that the old boy network was a *real* conspiracy. This idea that they are a 'mafia of the mediocre' is something that the old boys share with the freemasons.

14. Mangan, *Games Ethic*, 74.

15. The Bedales prospectus proclaimed: "Stemming from Badley's original intentions, the educational programme at Bedales goes some way to answer the complaint of E. M. Forster against the public schools of his day they they left their pupils with instructed brains and 'undeveloped hearts'." *Bedales School Prospectus*, Petersfield, 1985, 2. Abbotsholme is another example. Today the "alternative" schools seem tame, or to have been tamed.

16. In *The Guardians*, Philip Woodruff (Philip Mason) wrote: "I have long thought that the artistry with which he presents his arguments conceals for many people the horror of Plato's conclusions. He is, I believe, the father of Hegel and Nietzsche and of the Prussian and the Fascist state and I do not see how he can be absolved of some responsibility for Marxism, and

113

Whitemouth School, Manitoba. Highly irreverent, but perhaps indicating a good-humoured view of the whole business.

indeed for all theories of the state that equate us with ants and bees." Philip Woodruff, *The Men Who Ruled India: The Guardians*, Vol. 2, Jonathan Cape, 1953, 368.

17. "Colin Cowdrey", *The Tonbridgian*, Vol. LXXV, No. 688, Michaelmas Term 1985, 7.

18. R. F. Delderfield, *To Serve Them All My Days*, Hodder and Stoughton, 1980, 180.

19. University of California Press, Berkeley, 1983.

20. This flavoured Imperial historiography. In the Arabian Gulf the British partly justified their intervention on the grounds that they were protecting everyone from piracy, which in retrospect seems a trifle exaggerated.

114

The Imperial Grand Council of the Ancient Arabic Order of the Noble of the Mystic Shrine. An order proscribed by some grand lodges. Canadian members have included Prime Minister John Diefenbaker. The Shrine crescent is made of a Royal Bengal tiger's claws and the organization's obsessions with scimitars is also that of Saddam Hussein. He has erected Baghdad's answer to the Arc de Triomphe to commemorate his "victories" – huge crossed swords held by giant bronze fore-arms, reproducing a coat of arms that Saddam devised for himself.

CHAPTER SIX

THE PUBLIC SCHOOL PROBLEM

How was it, then, that the first, and for long the greatest, industrial power in the world came so to neglect its most important and only permanent asset, the capability of its own people? It had not been for lack of warning.

Correlli Barnett, *The Audit of War*, 1986.

The British relationship to Empire was unique, and they suffered for it. The Americans were not changed by their occupation of the Philippines, nor the Germans by their short empire in Africa. Other nations did not have cultures that incorporated their territorial expansion into a credo in the way that British culture incorporated the experience of Empire. If the British experience was so special, so too was the involvement of the schools.

Because the schools had been so closely connected with Imperialism, it was not surprising that as the Empire disappeared after World War II, the schools found themselves facing problems. The dissolution of the Empire meant a spiritual crisis for them, and they lost some of their legendary self-confidence.

Correlli Barnett for one blamed the Empire's dissolution squarely on them.[1] In fact, he singled out for particular blame Edward Thring, Uppingham's headmaster from 1853 until 1887.[2] Whether a single headmaster or a classroom full of headmasters could have prevented the Empire's decline is

115

Hale School, Western Australia. The black swan again, the state's ubiquitous symbol. The date is bogus but despite the jibes of historians, Hale clings to it.

dubious, but the alleged failure of the schoolmasters emphasizes that Imperialism involved more than economic exploitation.[3]

It would be easy to see the end of Empire as an inevitable realization that the Emperor had no clothes and that the rituals were just that and no more. Yet nostalgia (or the triumph of cultural hegemony) is often a puzzlement. Observers might be excused for wondering if the former British territories were left with only unhappy memories. The barristers' wigs and parliamentary maces did not disappear; the overseas public schools kept their uniforms and the freemasons kept their aprons.

British Week in the Arabian Gulf emirate of Qatar in 1986 is a case in point. Events included a Grand Opening of exhibits by His Grace The Duke of Wellington. He was touted as "Eton . . . Silver Stick-in-Waiting". The Duke was surrounded by Punch & Judy Shows, English Morris Dancers, and (next to the Ye Olde Worlde Sweet Shop) the Camelot Castle Supabounder. On display with him were replicas of the English Crown Jewels, the Robes of King Henry VIII and his six wives, and (near the Authentic Double Decker Bus) the Costumes of Robin Hood and His Merry Men.[4] The Ambassador to Qatar, Julian Walker (Old Bedfordian), who had been Political Agent on the Trucial Coast during more sedate days, commented that "at first the British were known to the Qataris for their navy . . .",[5] and observed hopefully that Britain was still "Qatar's major trading partner". [6]

When they won their freedom Britain's possessions usually did not opt for double decker buses or for an unreconstructed British system of education, but the Imperial legacy was not easily shaken off. For one thing, to change to a universal and comprehensive educational system would have cost substantial money. The comprehensive alternative on an American model was beyond the finances of many developing countries. There also was a lingering admiration for British standards of excellence and indeed for British ritualism.

116

Prince of Wales School, Vancouver. A presumably unauthorised use that affords a simple solution to the school's symbolism.

The Public School Problem

Injurious but not Malicious

In retrospect, if the public school influence was injurious, it was not maliciously so. What had been advocated was what the Imperial administrators knew. Part of their admiration for their public schools was of course because of their isolation overseas, cut off as they were from the familiarities of daily life at home. Loneliness had magnified the memory of their school days. Curzon viewed India with "tearful self-pity" because it would isolate him from his Eton chums. The old boys abroad became more devoted to their schools than their colleagues in England.[7]

As far as estimating the influence of the public school on the Imperial leadership, what else could have been so decisive in shaping men like Curzon? Birth in Scotland or the home counties? Religion? Marriage? It need only be asked concerning the importance of being an old boy: what if the moguls of Empire had gone to grammar schools?

Since the British departure, her former wards have striven to eradicate much of her influence, and much of what remains has been reduced to the banality of paste Crown Jewels. Even so, traces remain of the rituals fostered by the old boys. Like shells on the beach, silently testifying to former occupants, the talismans remained after Britain's departure.[8]

The social legacy can be a troublesome one. The public school was not the place to acquire an empathy for the masses. Ian Hansen wrote about the Australian public school, Camberwell, in the 1930s:

> Across the river from Camberwell, in Richmond and in Brunswick, the unemployed had declared the municipal sustenance rations black and demonstrated against their inability to obtain ration tickets redeemable at food stores: the handouts of bread and meat were an affront to the little dignity they had left. The major eye-sore in Melbourne was the Jolimont Reserve, where a thousand men slept under makeshift shelters on undrained ground that

117

Malvern College. One of the more basic of English public school coats.

became a quagmire after rain, from which they were turned out each day and where in the evening they lined up for stew and dry bread, bread and jam and cocoa. Camberwell Grammar School, within walking distance from Jolimont, over the Richmond Bridge, was in another world.[9]

If the public schools were abolished to help achieve equality, it seems unlikely that Etonians would troop to the nearest comprehensive school to assist in social integration. More likely was the suggestion that those schools that could would go into exile, and some Swiss valley would resound to "Well played!".

Full Circle

With the Empire gone, the debate continued and even seemed to move full circle. When liberalism was in vogue in the 1950s and 1960s, elitism was deplored, but then came a sea of change.[10] If the British had failed to make a success of comprehensive education and the independent system still discriminated in favour of the few, it was increasingly uncertain that equal access to an elitist education would be useful or welcome.

This impasse and non-solution was abetted by a new British conservatism, coupled with a genuine concern about the quality of education. The public schools warded off their enemies. Mrs. Thatcher's success at the polls assisted, but the best defence proved to be an offence fought under the banner of excellence. The schools' self-confidence was restored.

The turnabout crystallized in the Independent Schools' Information Service (ISIS), a coalition of independent school interests founded in 1972 "to inform the public of the true nature of independent schools and of their value to the nation". Shrewdly, the snobbish public schools were transformed into freedom-loving independent schools. Madison Avenue came to the rescue of Billy Bunter.

118

King's High School, Dunedin. An attractive New Zealand design with lion rampant.

The proliferation of science facilities, libraries, indoor swimming pools and other improvements was no less impressive than the psychological comeback. Millions of pounds going for computers and language laboratories. The up-dating of the physical plant was accompanied by revolutionary social changes. Fagging was abolished, the cane disappeared, and to the bewilderment of old boys, the all-male schools began admitting girls.

Any charge made about the schools' lack of pragmatism would have to stand up against the guerilla raid they carried out on the sixth forms of girls' schools. The formerly boys' schools discovered the virtues of co-education. In the face of this some headmistresses lost their gentility and described their male counterparts as "chauvinist pigs".

Although the headmasters sought absolution on the grounds that the girls' schools couldn't offer the academic advantages that the boys' schools could, the policy seemed to be more motivated by the bursar than by pedagogy. The advent of co-education, along with the other reforms, made the public schools considerably stronger as *educational* institutions than they had ever been before.

One of Its Leading Merits

Unfortunately for their partisans, doubts remain as to whether the schools are truly reformed as *ritualistic* institutions. Their totems seem still to be largely in place. On a Speech Day at St. Lawrence College, Alan Brown quoted ironically some Dickens:

> "Poor old Dr. Dombey said, 'I've been thinking of Dr. Blimber's (the next door establishment).' 'My neighbour, sir,' said Mrs. Pipchin. 'I believe the doctor's is an excellent establishment. I've heard that it is very strictly controlled and there's nothing but learning going on from morning to night.'" (Exactly like St. Lawrence College.) "'And it's very expensive,' added Dr. Dombey. 'And it's very

119

West Park School, Toronto. Writes Professor Campbell, "It is a sad commentary on the quality of imagination of Canadian educators that many schools use nothing more than an initial or monogram as an identifying symbol." State schools need to think about ritual.

expensive, sir,' returned Mrs. Pipchin, catching at the fact as if in omitting it she had omitted one of its leading merits." *May St. Lawrence flourish for ever.*[11]

To those who want the schools abolished, they remain the privileged passports to power,[12] and are responsible for perpetuation of the 'two nations'.[13] The Empire is gone, but because of the destruction of the direct-grant grammar schools and the doubts of parents about state education, the public schools in England enjoy an unprecedented prosperity. At whose expense this success has been produced is a problem. Gone are the dark days when the Labour government was openly considering how to nationalize them.[14] But could the opposition return?

A battle was won, but the war is far from over.[15] Unless Labour *never* returns to power, the public schools face an uncertain future. The only way the threat to them would completely vanish would be if the party system vanished. No rationalization can take away the fact that the influence of the schools is divisive. They reflect class divisions but they also through their ritualism help create class divisions.

Edmund King urged putting aside talk about the "performance" of public schools, conceding their merits, and asking about the other youth of England, "Did the children have a fair start?"[16] Most did not. Many do not. Those wishing to preserve the public schools must come to terms with the fact that they have been seen as so detrimental to British social cohesion that reasonable people would welcome their abolition. These are not people who are wild anarchists, but earnest men and women driven to despair by the class divisions in Britain.

Ticket of Admission

When the origins of Imperialism are laid bare, more will

Prince of Wales Lodge, Penang. A Malaysian lodge with forthright and self-explanatory symbolism.

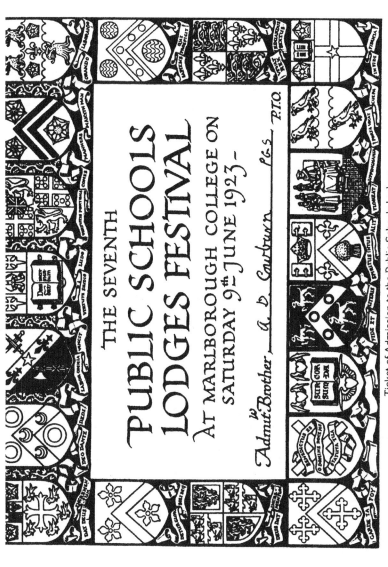

THE SEVENTH

PUBLIC SCHOOLS LODGES FESTIVAL

At Marlborough College on
Saturday 9th June 1923.

Admit Brother ___ A. D. Cockburn ___ P65

P.T.O.

Ticket of Admission to the Public Schools Lodges
Festival, 1923. In contrast with this heraldic
confidence of the public schools is the old and
humble seal of Louth Grammar School
(see Proverbs xiii:24, left).

A Lodge Initiation, 1890. The blindfolded candidate is about to be surprised. This is reminiscent of the incident in *Tom Brown's Schooldays*, when Tom as a new boy was initiated by being tossed "like a shuttlecock".

emerge about the schools as a wellspring of the ideology of Empire. This is a heavy burden in these egalitarian times. In some respects England is the last colony and the last victim of the old boy Imperialists. It is still necessary to have a ticket of admission to the upper reaches of British society. (See *Ticket of Admission to the Public Schools Lodges Festival, 1923*, page 121.) The initiation into upper class rituals still goes on. (See *Lodge Initiation*, page 122.) Indeed, if one compares the illustration on page 122 of a masonic initiation with illustrations of public school hazing, including the famous episode of blanket-tossing in *Tom Brown*, one hardly discerns a difference. The rites are somewhat less rude in these days, but equally important.

It is sad that, as a consequence, one proposed answer to England's educational problems is the destruction of schools whose history belongs not only to England but to the world. Despite the well-warranted criticisms, the public schools are in a number of ways of international significance. The part they have played in the history of countries other than Britain should be appreciated. Harrow is as much Nehru's school as Churchill's.

When Britain's former possessions can review their history more dispassionately, the public schools will be seen as fully as important to their past as to Britain's. But elitism is unacceptable in the present day. So for most countries, the pressures for an equalizing elixir outweigh excellence. Arthur Koestler noted: "To hope for salvation to be synthesized in the laboratory may seem materialistic, crankish or naive; it reflects the ancient alchemist's dream to concoct the *elixir vitae*."[17]

The transformation supposedly to be wrought by the destruction of the schools might prove as illusory as the permanence of the Empire did. A more constructive solution would be to look in the history of the public schools for directions that both friend and enemy could endorse. In the international associations which the public schools have had

123

Trowel. Ceremonially used by the Grand Lodge of Scotland to "spread the cement of brotherhood".

may be part of a solution. Few institutions have enjoyed longer associations with overseas education.

Based on this heritage, an increased involvement in multinational and multi-ethnic education could earn the respect of foes.[18] Schools open to the world in the best sense would not have to worry about their existence.

Reprieved

The public schools have not changed enough to guarantee their existence. They have been reprieved. Their present prosperity should not lull them into complacency. The problems they created persist. The public schools still perform in Britain something of the socially controlling role they used to perform in the Empire. However, they could be ritual-makers for a world community.

In a word, there should be no illusions about the changes that would be necessary before the schools redeem themselves in the eyes of their opposition. Nor should there be illusions about the latent strength of that opposition. There are today few votes for independent schools in Liverpool.

The schools' history could provide the key to their long-term preservation. There is no reason why there cannot be a cultural hegemony of human respect and understanding. Hegemony does not always have to be nefarious. Nor is there anything intrinsically bad about ritualism, which can unite people around democratic values just as well as it can around condescending ones.

True internationalization would make the public schools relevant to the twenty-first century. The opportunity that exists because of the current respite from political attack should not be lost. When all is said and done, the public schools are a unique cultural resource. Before they are again put against the wall, creative answers should be sought.

The Eastern Star. Widespread, but banned in some jurisdictions, this Masonic order admits both men and women.

NOTES—CHAPTER SIX

1. "Except for young Nazis or Communists," he wrote, "no class of leaders in modern times has been so subjected to prolonged moulding of character, personality and outlook at British public school boys . . ." Correlli Barnett, *The Collapse of British Power*, Morrow, 1972, 24.

2. In support of his case he quoted Thring: ". . . what is a nation doing which calmly stands up and says, 'We will only regard in our schools the breeding of the strong head; and we will give all power and honour to the wielders of strength'? This is but the Vandal all over again . . . glory to the strong on the reverse side of the shield is oppression to the weak . . . Alas for the many, alas for the pith, and working fibre of the nation; alas for all the gentler, and finer qualities by which society lives . . . All tender influences, all prevailing, patient, unpretending good may pack and be gone." Edward Thring, *Theory and Practice of Teaching*, Cambridge University Press, 1910, 36, qd. Barnett, *Collapse of British Power*, 29. Donald Leinster-Mackay challenges this view of Thring in *The Educational World of Edward Thring: A Centenary Study.*

3. Such charges, valid against some public school leaders, are not appropriately directed at Thring. He opposed the elitism of the Clarendon schools.

4. *Programme of Events*, British Fortnight, Doha, April 7-18, 1986.

125

Mill Hill. For some reason, birds in English public school heraldry often resemble pigeons and are remarkably plump. See page 31.

5. Indeed they were well known, since British warships bombarded the Qatari coast on a number of occasions.

6. *Programme*, British Fortnight.

7. "England and its allies defeated the Axis powers, but the Churchillians lost the empire. Its knell had tolled from time to time during the war, and Colville reveals that Churchill had not been deaf to it . . . On Aug. 30, 1941, Churchill learned that the Spitfires and Hawker Hurricanes that had won the Battle of Britain were piloted by students from state schools, not schoolboys from the elite private schools, (and) he said: 'They have saved this country; they have the right to rule it.'" William Manchester, "Downing Street Diarist: An Insider's Portrait of Churchill", rev. of *The Fringes of Power*, John Colville, Norton, 1985, in *International Herald Tribune*, October 22, 1985, 18.

8. A reminder appeared in the *Guardian*: "But now a certain breed of Briton that used to be pervasive is seen only rarely in such watering holes as the Nell Gwynne Pub at the Al Falaj Hotel (in Muscat). Walter Helfer, a German who ran Omani televison for two years after it started up in 1974, remembers the walrus-moustached former functionaries from British colonies long since granted independence. 'These guys were in their mid-forties, with no chance to go back to England and make a new life there,' Helfer recalled. 'You found people who defended, silently, the Empire. They were like a secret society. They were something straight from Kipling or Somerset Maugham.'" Christopher Dickey, "UK's Changing Role in Oman", *The Guardian Weekly*, Vol. 133, No. 21, 24 November 1985, 16.

9. Ian Hansen, *By Their Deeds: A Centenary History of Camberwell Grammar School, 1886-1986*, Canterbury (Victoria), 1986, 125.

10. About this change, affecting appraisal of the accomplishments of British overseas education, Warnock said: "But equality of opportunity is by no means the rallying cry that once it was.

Substitute Governor, Royal Order of Scotland. The governor of this Masonic order is the Monarch, if male, and a Mason. The last was Edward VIII.

Indeed, it is, at the time of writing, a suspect if not positively out-dated notion . . . the idea of equality of opportunity is particularly associated with the optimistic non-radical socialism of the 1940s . . . the very nature of education made it inappropriate to speak of it as a kind of uniform material like cake, to be handed out." Mary Warnock, *Schools of Thought*, Faber & Faber, 1977, 35.

11. Alan Brown (Fellow of Worcester College, Oxford), Chief Guest, Speechday 1972, *The Lawrentian*, Centenary Edition, 1979, Martell Press, Cliftonville, Kent, 79.

12. Christopher Lehmann-Haupt, "Preparing for Power", *International Herald Tribune*, 24-25 December 1985, 3.

13. T. J. H. Bishop, who with Rupert Wilkinson studied the Wykehamists in *Winchester and the Public School Elite*, wrote to the *Guardian* in 1985: "My judgment, for what it may be worth, is that "gentrification" has damaged and continues to damage our economy . . . (because) Winchester and public schools like Winchester still function as mechanisms of "social immobility", continuing to make it much less likely that others, not to the manner born—and many women inside as well as outside the charmed circle—will reach their well-merited places in our decision-making elites, right across our steadily declining economy." T. J. H. Bishop, "How a gentrifying diet leads to constipation", *The Guardian Weekly*, Vol. 133, No. 24, 15 December 1985, 2.

14. John Rae, "New Life for the Old School", *The Times*, 14 December 1985, 8. Rae, Headmaster of Westminster, wrote: "I joined the Headmasters Conference at this time and I recall the mood of defeatism. It was like finding yourself in a besieged town on the point of surrender: public talk about the need to collaborate with the enemy and private plans for *sauve qui peut*." *Ibid.*

15. Rae remarks: "In the new political climate, the independent schools pulled off a notable coup. They persuaded the

127

Winchester. A design reflecting its High Victorian origins: "quotidian reinforcement of behaviour by nobiliary icons".

Conservatives to launch the assisted places scheme to give some poorer children an independent education. The scheme did extend choice but only in the sense that two extra lifeboats would have extended choice aboard the Titanic. A few more children were enabled to escape the sinking ship, but what happened to those left behind did not appear to concern the independent sector . . ." *Ibid.*

16. King, *Other Schools and Ours*, 239. The answer, King strongly suggested, was *no*. For all the effort, in 1971 when about 28% of the boys leaving public schools went up to university in Britain, only one boy out of a thousand was entering university from secondary modern school and *one girl out of twelve thousand*. King simply adds: "This personal doom for so many became a national disaster—socially, technologically, and educationally." *Ibid.*, 238.

17. *Ibid.*, 106.

18. Lord Mountbatten's enthusiasm for the Atlantic Colleges scheme, and Sevenoaks School's international boarding house, are examples of an interest in seeing schools acquire a more diverse, multi-racial, multi-national, student body.

Royal Arch Apron. The Royal Arch is one of the most frequently given optional series of degrees after the obligatory first three, and makes much use of the triple tau cross. (See page 91).

The Earl of Zetland as The Most Worshipful Grand
Master. Lord Zetland was elected Grand Master
of the United Grand Lodge of England in 1844 in
succession to HRH The Duke of Sussex. He was
succeeded by the Marquess of Ripon in 1870, who
resigned in 1874 on becoming Roman Catholic
and was succeeded by the Prince of Wales
(Edward VII).

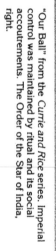

"Our Ball" from the *Currie and Rice* series. Imperial control was maintained by ritual and its social accoutrements. The Order of the Star of India, right.

BIBLIOGRAPHY

Unless otherwise stated, books in this bibliography were published in London. If a paperback edition is available and suitable, it is listed. Not all texts cited in the footnotes are listed, this being a select list of materials considered to be useful.

1. BOOKS

Albertini, Rudolf von, *European Colonial Rule, 1880-1940: The Impact of the West on India, Southeast Asia, and Africa*, Clio Press, Oxford, 1982.

Al-Tall, Ahmad Yousef, *Education in Jordan*, National Book Foundation, Islamabad, 1979.

Allen, Charles and Sharada Dwivedi, *Lives of the Indian Princes*, Arrow/Century Hutchinson, 1986.

Allen, Charles, ed., *Plain Tales from the Raj: Images of British India in the Twentieth Century*, Futura, 1985.

Allen, Charles, *Tales from the South China Seas: Images of the British in South-East Asia in the Twentieth Century*, Futura, 1985.

Armstrong, John A., *The European Administrative Elite*, Princeton University Press, 1973.

Tribal Gods – national symbols for which men would die – of the 19th century. Left to right; John Bull, Britannia, Germania, France and Cathleen in Houlihan.

Ayres, Eric, *Woodbridge School: An Outline History*, Woodbridge School, Ipswich, 1962.

Badger, Alfred B., *The Public Schools and The Nation*, Robert Hale, 1944.

Baker, Nigel, ed., *Truro School Centenary, 1880-1980*, Blackfords Press, Truro, 1980.

Bamford, T. W., *Rise of the Public Schools: a study of boys' public schools in England and Wales from 1837 to the present day*, Nelson, 1967.

Barnett, Correlli, *The Collapse of British Power*, Morrow, 1972.

Barr, Ann & Peter York, *The Official Sloane Ranger Diary*, Ebury Press, 1983.

Bello, Alhaji Sir Ahmadu, *My Life*, Cambridge University Press, 1962.

Bok, Sissela, *Secrets: On the Ethics of Concealment and Revelation*, Oxford University Press, 1986.

Bradley, John, ed., *Lady Curzon's India: Letters of a Vicereine*, Widenfeld and Nicolson, 1985.

Bolton, W. F., *The Language of 1984*, Blackwell, Oxford, 1984.

Braibanti, Ralph, *Asian Bureaucratic Systems Emergent from the British Imperial Tradition*, Duke University Press, Durham (North Carolina), 1966.

Brown, Aggrey, *Color, Class, and Politics in Jamaica*, Transaction Books, New Brunswick, New Jersey, 1979.

Busch, Briton Cooper, *Britain and the Persian Gulf, 1894-1914*, University of California Press, Berkeley, 1967.

Heraldic Coronets indicating rank. Everyone in the Empire had their assigned place and the assigned symbols to indicate that place.

Bibliography

Chandos, John, *Boys Together: English Public Schools 1800-1864*, Oxford University Press, 1985.

Christie-Murray, David, *Armorial Bearings of British Schools*, W. Heffer & Sons, Cambridge, nd.

Collenette, V. G., *Elizabeth College*, Guernsey Press, St. Peter Port, 1963.

Curtin, Philip D., ed., *Imperialism*, Macmillan, 1971.

Delderfield, R. F., *To Serve Them All My Days*, Hodder and Stoughton, 1980.

Dennis, Rodney, *Heraldry and the Heralds*, Jonathan Cape, 1982.

Dewar, James, *The Unlocked Secret: Freemasonry Examined*, William Kimber, 1986.

Dickson, Violet, *Forty Years in Kuwait*, George Allen & Unwin, 1971.

Duggan, William Redman, *Our Neighbors Upstairs: The Canadians*, Nelson-Hall, Chicago, 1979.

Eldridge, C. C., *British Imperialism in the Nineteenth Century*, Hodder & Stoughton, 1978.

Falkus, Malcolm & John Gillingham, *Historical Atlas of Britain*, Granada, 1981.

Forster, E. M., *A Passage to India*, Abinger Edition, 1979.

Gerstenberg, Frank, *Oswestry School—575 Years*, Countryside Publications, Chorley, 1982.

Gopal, Sarvepalli, *Jawaharial Nehru*, Volume I, Oxford University Press, Delhi, 1975.

King Edward VII School, South Africa. On Edward's death Johannesberg College was allowed to adopt his name and to adopt suitably. commemorative arms.

Graham, Sonia F., *Government and Mission Education in Northern Nigeria, 1900-1919, with special reference to the work of Hanns Vischer*, Ibadan University Press, Ibadan, 1966.

Gray, Herbert Branston, *The Public Schools and the Empire*, Williams & Norgate, 1913.

Guttsman, W. L., ed., *The English Ruling Class*, Widenfield and Nicolson, 1969.

Hall, H. L., *Meliorsora Sequamur, Brighton Grammar School, 1882-1982*, Brighton Grammar School, Brighton (Victoria), 1983.

Hansen, Ian V., *By Their Deeds: A Centenary History of Camberwell Grammar School, 1886-1986*, Camberwell Grammar School, Canterbury (Victoria), 1986.

Heald, Tim, *Networks*, Hodder and Stoughton, 1983.

Heeney, Brian, *Mission to the Middle Classes: the Woodard Schools, 1848-1891*, SPCK, 1969.

Henderson, K. W., *Masonic World Guide*, Lewis Masonic, 1984.

Henn, Wilfred E., *A Life So Rich: being a biography of The Rev. Canon P. U. Henn*, Perth (Australia), 1982.

Hobson, J. A., *Imperialism: A Study*, Third Edition, George Allen & Unwin, 1961.

Holmes, Brian, *Comparative Education: Some Considerations of Method*, George Allen & Unwin, 1981.

Honey, J. R., de S., *Tom Brown's Universe: The Development of the Victorian Public School*, Millington, 1977.

134

Jewel of a Masonic Knight Companion of the Red Cross of Constantine. The order also confers the Knighthoods of the Holy Sepulchre and of St. John. Masonry became an alternative Imperial honours system.

Bibliography

Hughes, Judith, *Emotion and High Politics: Personal Relations at the Summit in Late Nineteenth-Century Britain and Germany*, University of California Press, Berkeley, 1983.

Hyam, Ronald, *Britain's Imperial Century, 1815-1914: A Study of Empire and Expansion*, B&N, 1976.

King, Edmund J., *Other Schools and Ours: comparative studies for today*, Fifth Edition, Holt, Rinehart and Winston, 1979.

Koestler, Arthur, *Janus: a summing up*, Picador, 1983.

Laver, James, *The Book of Public School Old Boys, University, Navy, Army, Air Force & Club Ties*, Seeley, 1968.

Leinster-Mackay, Donald, *The Rise of the English Prep School*, The Falmer Press, 1984.

Leinster-Mackay, Donald, *The Educational World of Edward Thring*, The Falmer Press, 1987.

Macaulay, G. A., *Schoolroom and Playing Field: A Centernnial History of Timaru Boys' High School, 1880-1980*, Timaru Herald, Timaru (New Zealand), 1980.

McGregor, G. P., *King's College Budo: The First Sixty Years*, Oxford University Press, Nairobi, 1967.

Mack, Edward C., *Public Schools and British Opinion Since 1860*, Columbia University Press, 1941 (reprinted Greenwood Press, Westport, 1971).

Maguire, Patrick, *A Brief Sketch of Development at Cranleigh*, Cranleigh School, nd.

Mangan, J. A., *Athleticism in the Victorian and Edwardian Public School*, Cambridge University Press, 1981.

The Orphic Egg. The egg represents the soul of the seeker and the serpent represents the Mysteries. Quite apart from the baubles that Masonry conferred was the prospect held out of philosophic regeneration.

Mangan, J. A., *The Games Ethic and Imperialism*, Viking, Harmondsworth, 1986.

Mansfield, Bruce, *Knox: A History of Knox Grammar School, 1924-1974*, Knox Grammar School, Sydney (Australia), 1974.

Mason, Philip, *A Shaft of Sunlight*, Andre Deutsch, 1978.

Morris, James, *Farewell the Trumpets: An Imperial Retreat*, Penguin Books, Harmondsworth, 1984.

Morris, James, *Pax Britannica: The Climax of an Empire*, Penguin Books, Harmondsworth, 1984.

Nadel, George H., and Perry Curtis, eds., *Imperialism and Colonialism*, Macmillan, 1964.

Nemeth, Thomas, *Gramsci's Philosophy*, Harvester Press, Brighton, 1980.

Quigley, Carroll, *The Anglo-American Establishment: From Rhodes to Cliveden*, Books in Focus, New York, 1981.

Quigly, Isabel, *The Heirs of Tom Brown: The English School Story*, Oxford University Press, 1984.

Record, S. P., *Proud Century: the first hundred years of Taunton School*, E. Goodman, Taunton, 1948.

Rose, Kenneth, *Curzon: A Most Superior Person*, Macmillan, 1985.

Said, Edward W., *Orientalism*, Routledge & Kegan Paul, 1978.

Schumpeter, Joseph A., *Imperialism and Social Classes*, Basil Blackwell, Oxford, 1951.

Sharp, John, *Educating One Nation*, Max Parrish, 1959.

136

Cheltenham. Public schools issued pocket sized calendars for each term, often with a version of the arms on their covers.

Bibliography

Singh, R. P., *The Indian Public School*, Sterling Publishers, New Delhi, 1972.

Smith, W. O., *To Whom Do Schools Belong*, Basil Blackwell, Oxford, 1942.

Spangenberg, Bradford, *British Bureaucracy in India: Status, Policy and the Indian Civil Service in the late 19th Century*, South Asis Books, Columbia, 1976.

Stone, Lawrence, and Jeanne C. Fawtier Stone, *An Open Elite? England 1540-1880*, Abridged Edition, Oxford University Press, 1986.

Symonds, Richard, *The British and Their Successors: A Study in the Development of the Government Services in the New States*, Faber and Faber, 1966.

Thornton, A. P., *The Imperial Idea and Its Enemies*, Second Edition, Macmillan, 1985.

Tidrick, Kathryn, *Heart-beguiling Araby*, Cambridge University Press, 1981.

Ward, J. F., *Prince Alfred College: The story of the first eighty years, 1869-1949*, Prince Alfred College, Adelaide (Australia), 1951.

Warnock, Mary, *Schools of Thought*, Faber & Faber, 1977.

Whiting, Audry, *The Kents*, Futura, 1985.

Winks, Robin W., ed., *British Imperialism: Gold, God, Glory*, Holt, Rinehart and Winston, New York, 1963.

Wood, Anthony, *Nineteenth Century Britain*, Second Edition, Longman, Harlow, 1982.

Indian Blue Ensign Badge. Ties between branches of Imperial symbolism remain uninvestigated, e.g. the badge of a knight grand commander of the Star of India was used by at least one Masonic lodge and on the Blue Ensign by ships in the Indian Marine.

Woodruff, Philip, *The Founders*, Vol. I & II, Jonathan Cape, 1953. Philip Woodruff is the pen name of Philip Mason.

Zartman, Ira William, ed., *Elites in the Middle East*, Praeger, New York, 1980.

Zijderveld, Anton C., *The Abstract Society: A Cultural Analysis of Our Time*, Penguin Books, Harmondsworth, 1974.

2. PERIODICALS, SERIALS, YEARBOOKS

Allhallow School Year Book, Allhallow School.

The American Historical Review.

Ampleforth Journal, Ampleforth School.

Ars Quatuor Coronatorum.

Bulletin, Wanganui Collegiate School, New Zealand.

The Corian, Geelong Grammar School Quarterly.

Daedalus, journal of the American Academy.

The Financial Times.

The Guardian.

The Guardian Weekly.

The Heraldry Gazette, Official Newsletter of the Heraldry Society.

International Herald Tribune.

Khaleej Times, Dubai, United Arab Emirates.

Illegal Arms, City of Zion, Illinois. The arms and seal mentioning God and displaying a cross were ruled illegal by the courts in 1990 for violating the American Constitution's separation of church and state.

Bibliography

The Lawrentian, St. Lawrence School, Ramsgate.

Middle East Research and Information Reports, New York.

The Ousel, magazine of Bedford School.

Public & Preparatory Schools Yearbook, Adam & Charles Black.

The Radleian, Radley School.

The Rugby Meteor, Rugby School.

The Tonbridgian, Tonbridge School.

The Times.

Times Educational Supplement.

Trinity College School News, Trinity College, Ontario.

3. UNPUBLISHED SOURCES

India Office Records, The India Office Library, London. Some of the privately issued masonic histories in the Grand Lodge Library, London, are produced by photocopied typescript.

Three Pillars of Freemasonry. In the rituals, architecture was invested with meaning – in this case wisdom, strength and beauty – so that buildings teach part of the covert teachings.

Garden Party in honour of the Prince of Wales, at Belvedere, Calcutta. Edward's
1875-1876 visit was followed by the brilliant heraldry and ceremonial of the
Imperial Assemblage held at Delhi in 1877 proclaiming Queen Victoria
as Empress of India (See page 33).

INDEX

Prepared by Elizabeth Wallis

142

Queen's College, Hong Kong. This prominent boy's public school was established in 1862.

Index

The Flag Research Center, Winchester, Massachusetts. Vexillology, the study of flags, overlaps with heraldry. The literature of both, along with that of Masonry, remains unexplored by historians of education.

144

Heraldry is quite capable of being contemporary, as the arms of the United Kingdom Atomic Energy Authority illustrate – the motto translates "Out of the least the greatest". The supporting pantheons are rare creatures that always appear spangled with stars, whose points in this design add up to ninety-two, the number of electrons in uranium.

Marks of cadency for male children. Each boy thus could be heraldrically labelled.

146

Society for Creative Anachronism. This new and fast-growing organization recalls the Victorian revival of chivalry and heraldry: members take archaic names and contend for dukedoms and baronies in kingdoms that have been created throughout the world.

Index

King's School, Canterbury. Compare with the arms of King's School, Parramatta, page 45.

148

Badge of Beaumont. An example of elephant and castle heraldry from Canterbury Cathedral, c. 1410 see page 34.

Plumed helmet for Indian Army Officers. This popular model came from George Kenning, Aldersgate Street, London. Kenning was a major supplier as well of cocked hats.

Masonic square and compass. The positioning enabled the brethen to know which degree was in process.

Index

151

Resurrection of Masonic Initiate. The candidate in the third degree, just prior to resurrection by the Masonic Grip.

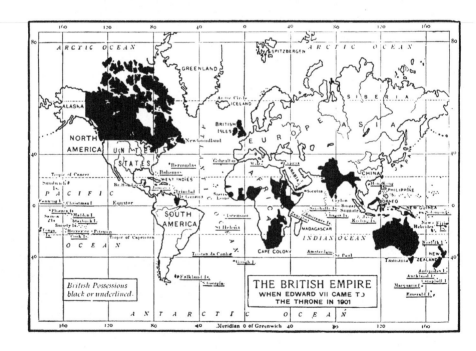

THE BRITISH EMPIRE
WHEN EDWARD VII CAME TO THE THRONE IN 1901

British Possessions black or underlined.

Interior of the Heralds College.

Printed in Great Britain
by Amazon

79873774R00098